Morning Reflections
ON THE Song
OF Solomon

The Mystery of the Bride and Groom

LORRIE BELKE
MARLENE BERGMAN

ISBN 978-1-64140-435-8 (paperback)
ISBN 978-1-64140-436-5 (digital)

Christian Faith Publishing, Inc.
832 Park Avenue
Meadville, PA 16335
www.christianfaithpublishing.com

Printed in the United States of America

Table of Contents

DEDICATION

This book is dedicated to Tobias Schmidt, a special needs son of a minister. A portion of the proceeds of this book will go to Toby's living and medical expenses.

Lorrie

Preface

This devotional is written to the Body of Christ as well as those who are seeking and considering a relationship with the Lord. For those of you who are wondering what a relationship with Jesus is like, this book will aid you in your fellowship and search to know Him more intimately.

The Song of Solomon is a story of love - an allegory of God's love for Israel, and a pattern of Christ's love for the Church. For individual believers, this book leads one into a deeper communion with Jesus Christ, the lover of their soul.

In Matthew 25:6 Jesus talks about the *Parable of the Ten Virgins*. The ten virgins were waiting for the bridegroom to arrive. There were five foolish and five wise, but the Word says they *all* fell asleep. Only the five wise virgins were sufficiently prepared and had oil in their lamps. The five foolish virgins did not have sufficient oil and were told by the wise virgins to return to the city and buy oil for themselves. When they left to go and get oil, they missed the coming of the bridegroom. The door was shut and they missed their window of opportunity. We must all be prepared and ready because no one knows the day or the hour when the Son of man will return! My prayer for you, is that you will be amongst the wise, prepared children of God!

Knowing that the Parable of the Ten Virgins is about the return of Jesus Christ, the five virgins waiting with sufficient oil speaks of a bride (Church) that is ready for the return of Jesus Christ. She has regularly spent time with Him, she is filled with the Holy Spirit (oil), and she knows her Lord and Savior intimately.

May this book lead you into a closer intimate relationship with Jesus, the lover of your soul - your soon coming King!

- Rev. Danette J. Crawford
  Founder and President
  Danette Crawford Ministries
  Joy Ministries Evangelistic Association

Introduction

The image of God is in your soul. Its nature may be learnt from its renewal by Christ.[1] Before the fall, the image of God in man was perfect. Now, because of Christ the image of God in us is restored. One may mirror this divine glory. Even though the first estate was lost through Adam, Christ has saved us from a fearful deformity. Paul commends us to "put on the new man, who after God is created in righteousness and true holiness" (Eph. 4:24).

We are called to put on the new man, made in the image of our Creator, clothed with flesh, we are His people called by His name. Because of Jesus Christ we are "restored to true and substantial integrity."[2] But how do we become like Him, if we do not read His Word and pray?

We are loved with an everlasting love. Through the providence of God, He watches over us. He has numbered the hairs of our head. We are called the "children of God," and we are referred to in scripture as "His bride."

Morning Reflections on the Song of Solomon is written for those who already know Jesus Christ, and for those who are interested in learning more about Him. Some are ready for the return of Jesus, their bridegroom, while others are waiting for

---

1   John Calvin, *The Institutes of the Christian Religion, Ed.* Henry Beveridge (Seattle, Washington: Pacific Publishing Studio, 2011), 92.
2   Ibid, 94.

His return, but their oil has run out. Some do not have a full supply of oil to keep their lamps lit.

Spending time with Jesus daily is of prime importance because we want to become more like Him and learn of Him. When we spend time with Jesus in his Word and prayer, we can learn of Him and His ways. In His presence there is fullness of joy. In His presence our oil is replenished. We are filled.

Decide each morning to spend time with Jesus, to sit in His presence. Shut your door and shut the world out for just a few minutes every day. When you do, lists will present themselves to your mind. For lists and things that come to your mind, write them down so you can do them later. Once you have placed your concern on paper, you can rest your mind. Turn your paper over and stop reviewing your list.

Early morning is the best time to meet with Jesus, before the family wakes up. You are fresh from a good night's sleep, and you have decided to spend your waking half hour or hour with the captain of your heart, the lover of your soul. If you can only sit still for ten minutes, start with something, and eventually your time with Him will grow.

Jesus calls you. Perhaps you have resisted and no longer hear His voice. You long to experience His presence and hear His voice again. I cannot promise you that you will feel His presence immediately or hear His voice, but I know that He is faithful to come to His beloved ones.

Playing music softly in the background might be a good way to begin, but sometimes I listen more to the worship song and begin singing along, forgetting to quiet myself before the Lord.

You trust Jesus. You have repented of your sin and given your heart to Him. You have made Him Lord of your life and you are born again. Some may be desiring to know Jesus and desiring to give your heart to Him. Jesus will come to fellowship with you as you quiet yourself and begin talking with Him. If you need to repent of any sin, begin by telling Jesus today.

There is nothing else in this world that takes the place of fellowship with Jesus. His presence is magnificent.

You will experience joy as you quiet yourself and meditate on His Word. Greater joy will come as you are obedient to His Word. If you have pushed Him aside because you have been busy for a season, don't give up, but wait a few minutes until you sense His presence again. He is always available to fellowship with you. Be patient.

What is your priority today? To spend the first minutes of your day with Jesus? Then do it. Decide to spend time with Him and in His Word. Talk to Him like he is sitting in the room with you.

Morning Reflections on the Song of Solomon was written for you, to encourage you in a deeper walk with Jesus and a deeper Christian life. Ask the Holy Spirit to guide you and teach you about what you read in His Word. Ask Jesus to come and reside with you. Speak your prayers out loud. Read out loud if it will help you focus.

INTRODUCTION

In the words of E. C. Hadley,

> True Christianity is not a head knowledge of certain
> doctrines, but an intimate acquaintance with the living,
> loving Son of God. Alas, how many Christians seem sat-
> isfied with knowing that their sins are forgiven through
> His death, and fail to go on in fellowship with the living
> Son of God, whose love is better than wine. How much
> they lose in their own souls, for there is nothing that can
> compensate for lack of personal communion with the
> Lord. A soul that has been washed in the Blood of Christ
> can never be satisfied with anything short of personal
> intimate fellowship with Him.[3]

There are four views of the Song of Solomon. The first view
is the "glory of wedded love."[4] Second, the traditional view of
the Song of Solomon, is an allegory. The divine theme is dis-
guised in the picture of human love. "The lover is not a rustic
swain – it is Yahweh himself and the beloved maiden is Israel,
chosen by Yahweh as His bride."[5]

The third view of the Song of Solomon is that the marriage
bond used in Scripture is a pattern, a typology, of Christ and
the Church. The Song of Solomon portrays this relationship on
highest levels of devotion between Christ and the Church.

---

[3]   E.C. Hadley, *The Song of Solomon*, (Danville, Illinois: Grace & Truth, 1975), 3.
[4]   J. Vernon McGee, *Guidelines for the Understanding of Scriptures: Song of Solomon*, (TN: Thomas Nelson, 1988), 4.
[5]   Morris Jastrow, Jr., *The Song of Songs: Being A Collection of Love Lyrics of Ancient Palestine (Philadelphia:* J. B. Lippincott Company, 1921), 30.

The fourth, explained by McGee, depicts the communion of Christ and the individual believer. Here, the soul's communion with Christ is set forth.[6]

An allegory imposes a deeper, hidden, or spiritual meaning on the text. "Typology recognizes the validity of the Old Testament account in its own right, but then finds in that account a clear, parallel link with some event or teaching in the New Testament which the Old Testament account foreshadows."[7]

John of Ford (AD 1140-1244) so unmistakably illuminates that the "Old Testament bond between God and the unfaithful Jewish people (a bond that rested on the justice of the Law and was rescinded by Christ) is implicitly contrasted with the new marriage between Christ and the Church of the Gentiles, a bond resting on grace and love."[8]

This book is written for the bride, to instill in you His great, intimate love for you. As you begin your study, cherish a spirit of meditation as you set aside the things of the world. Then you will enjoy a rich blessing.

---

[6]   J. Vernon McGee, *Guidelines for the Understanding of Scriptures: Song of Solomon,* (TN; Thomas Nelson, 1988), 4.

[7]   Lloyd G. Carr, *The Song of Solomon: An Introduction and Commentary,* ed. D.J. Wiseman (Downers Grove, Illinois: InterVarsity Press, 1984), 23.

[8]   John of Ford, *Sermons of the Final Verses of the Song of Songs,* (Kalamazoo, Michigan:* Cistercian Publications, 1977-1984), 26.

For a King to be genuinely in love with His Bride offers truths that need to be shared.

As you read the Song of Solomon each day, may you accept God's love for you there.

Open your heart to receive God's love. Open your mind to prayerfully learn.

Open your lips to sing His Praise as you bask in God's love never earned!

The Mystery of the Bride and the Groom[9]

The ancient Jewish marriage has a tradition similar to the Song of Solomon. Before the bridegroom marries the bride, he has to journey from his house to her house. There he would pledge his love for her, consecrate his life, and give an expensive gift. The two would drink wine and celebrate their covenant. He would then return home and prepare his home for his bride.

During the time of separation, she would prepare herself. When the wedding day arrived, there would be a great procession. The bridegroom, dressed as a king, would arrive at night, carrying torches, bringing his men with him. The bride, dressed as a queen in wedding garments would be ready.

There would be a procession from her house to his house, and the celebration would last for seven days.

The mystery is that God is the bridegroom. We are His bride. The bridegroom made a journey from His house in heaven to our house here in earth about 2000 years ago. No matter where we are, He comes to us. He comes to the door of our hearts and we let Him in.

The costly treasure that the bridegroom paid was not of silver or gold but the price of His life. This is the bridal gift that

---

9   Jonathan Cahn, *The Book of Mysteries*, (Lake Mary, Florida: FrontLine, 2016), 118, 228.

set us free. He shares the cup of wine with us. Then He says He must return to His Father's house. He promises, "In my Father's house are many mansions: if it were not so, I would have told you. I go to prepare a place for you. And if I go and prepare a place for you, I will come again, and receive you unto myself; that where I am, there ye may be also" (John 14:2, 3). We are presently living in the time of separation. We are His bride.

He is in heaven at the right hand of the Father. We are here on earth, preparing ourselves for the marriage supper of the Lamb, and to live eternally in our new home with Him.

The day of Jesus Christ's return is His second visitation. He will return for us, whether we are alive on that day or whether we have lived our life, Jesus returns for His bride.

We will be carried away with Him and the great procession will begin. The old house will be left behind and we will enter heaven, the house of our bridegroom. This is the home we have dreamed of, and finally we will be home.

Welcome Heaven-bound Shulamites

"The soul must always have a heavenly vision to draw it out of itself, and away from the things of the earth."[10]

[10] Jessie Penn-Lewis, *Thy Hidden Ones: The life of the believer as illustrated in the Song of Solomon,* (Fort Washington, Pennsylvania: Christian Literature Crusade, 1899), 2.

$$Chapter\ 1$$

The Song of Solomon

1 The Song of Songs, which is Solomon's.

This book is the most amazing of 1005 songs (1 Kings 4:32) because the writer was anointed by the Holy Spirit. Therefore, it has its right place in the canon of scripture. Luther writes that it is "the chief or finest song."[11] It is named the Song of Songs because it is the "best" song. The word "song" means a joyful, festival song.

> Love always fills us with music. There are over 100 songs here to sing.
> Absorb God's loving musical caresses. Welcome the joy His Love Songs bring.
>
>

"The Song is found in the third section of the Hebrew Bible – the *Ketuvim* (Writings or Hagiographa) a miscellany including Wisdom literature, poetry, and history – that was granted

---

[11] Martin Luther, *History of the Great Reformation of the Sixteenth Century in Germany, Switzerland & C.*, Trans. J. H. Merle D'Aubigne. (New York: Robert Carter, 1846), 188.

canonical status centuries after the Torah and Prophets."[12] Approximately AD 135, Rabbi Akiva was instrumental in having the Song of Songs admitted into the canon. He insisted that the Song of Songs should be read allegorically:

> God forbid! No man in Israel ever disputed the status of the Song of Songs... For the whole world is not worth the day on which the Song of Songs was given to Israel; for all the writings are holy, but the Song of Songs is the holiest of the holy.[13]

As described earlier, The Song of Solomon is not only a love song written by King Solomon for His bride but also a spiritual allegory wherein there is the typology representing "a type of our Lord, the true Prince of peace"[14] and His chosen people—Christ and his church.

The bridegroom is Christ, and He loves His bride. He covers all her defects, and He rejoices over her. The bride refers to Christ as, "My beloved."

There are different voices in The Song of Solomon, like in a play, and they are as follows:

---

[12] Ariel Bloch and Chana Bloch, *The Song of Songs*, (Los Angeles: University of California Press, 1995), 28.

[13] Sid Z. Leiman, *The Canonization of Hebrew Scripture: The Talmudic and Midrashic Evidence* (New Haven: Transactions of the Connecticut Academy of Arts and Sciences, 1991), 121.

[14] James Hudson Taylor, *Union and Communion: Or Thoughts on the Song of Solomon* (Edinburgh: R. & R Clark, Ltd., 1914), 3.

- The Shulamite
- A chorus of the daughters of Jerusalem
- The Shepherd King
- The Bridegroom King
- The Shulamite bride

Each section is depicted in bold to designate who is speaking. This is not an addition to the scripture, but to aid in understanding. There are times when commentaries and theologians do not agree with one another. So, my recommendation is that you let the Holy Spirit guide you.

The Shulamite

2 Let him kiss me with the kisses of his mouth: for thy love is better than wine.

> Kisses involve loving action. Kisses are personalized and sweet.
>
> To be lovingly kissed by your Bridegroom is proof that two hearts did meet!
>
> Lord, help us to be aware of the many tokens of Your love to us today.
>
> Help us to accept the intimacy that flows from Your hand many ways.
>
>

Shulamite is a young maiden from Shulem or Shunem. The root word of Shulem is Salem and is from the Hebrew root שלמ shalom. Shulem or Shunem was a village belonging to the tribe of Issachar, the country of a certain Abishag the Shunammite.[15]

Shulamite means *peaceable* and *perfect*,[16] and the first part of Shulamite is pronounced Salem or Shalem. An alternate form of the Gentile name Shunamite refers to the inhabitants of Shunem (1 Kings 13:5). It is written either Shunamite or Shulamite, both are correct. "There is an interchange between the ל (l) and the נ (n), common in the Semitic languages."[17] An alternate form of spelling is Shulammite.

From here on, the young maiden will be called *Shulamite.*

The *Hebrew* name Solomon שְׁלֹמֹה (Shelomoh) was derived from *Hebrew* שלמ (shalom), meaning *peace*. Shulamite has some of the same letters in her name as does Solomon.

Here, in verse 2, Shulamite is talking to the king about her shepherd lover (v 2–4a). As we read on, we will understand that her shepherd lover is her shepherd king. He is one and the same.

She is peaceful. Not only does her name denote peaceful, but also that is who she is. The Shulamite desires His kiss, and she proclaims her love for the bridegroom. She yearns for His continual demonstration of affection towards her.

---

15   Ernest Renan, *The Song of Songs* (Paternoster Square, E. C. London: Mathieson & Co., 1860), 31.
16   W. Hall Harris, Daniel B. Wallace and Robert B. Chisholm, NET Bible. Ed. W. Hall Harris (Garland, Texas: Biblical Studies Press, 2005), passim.
17   Ibid.

His love and display of affection are more to be desired than anything else on the earth. Bernard of Clairvaux explains concerning the kiss more in depth:

> Not to all men does it belong to take these words upon their lips with sincere desire; he alone is able to do so, who has received even once only, the spiritual kiss from the lips of Christ; him his own experience incessantly urges to obtain a renewal of that which he found so full of sweetness. It is my strong opinion that no one can comprehend what it is, save he who has experienced it; it is, as it were, a hidden manna; and he who tastes of it, still hungers for it again. It is a fountain sealed from which no stranger may draw; but he who drinks of it still thirsts to drink again.[18]

A kiss is extremely intimate. The very breath of each is exchanged. And just as God breathed into Adam, he became a living soul. Here, we see that the bridegroom passes His Spirit of life into the Shulamite, and His life-giving breath by way of a kiss is better than wine.

> "All scripture is given by inspiration of God, and is profitable for doctrine, for reproof, for correction, for instruction in righteousness" (2 Tim. 3:16).

---

[18] Bernard of Clairvaux, *Life and Works of Saint Bernard: Eighty Six Sermons on The Song of Solomon*, Ed. John Mabillon (London: John Hodges, 1896), 17.

Here, *inspiration* means the breath of God.

Breathe on me breath of God,
Fill me with life anew,
That I may love what thou dost love,
And do what thou wouldst do.
(Edwin Hatch 1878)

She compares His kisses to wine. Wine in Jesus' day is served at a wedding feast. Here, wine makes people happy, but it is only for a few hours and then the effect wears off. Shulamite desires His love and desires Him more than the temporary effect that wine gives. She knows she can give her heart to Him, and He will be there for her. His love is not temporary. It is not fleeting. Wine can also deaden pain, if only for a few hours. But when her lover comes to her, His love removes all pain. In His presence, all pain is gone.

There are tremendous sensations of love that our hearts feel for our Lord. Joy, happiness, peace, and a deep, deep love that we experienced the day we were born again and experienced new life in Christ Jesus. We need to nourish and tend to this love so that it does not become like a stagnant pool of water but a fresh-flowing stream.

Many have experienced the loss of love in the natural or a love that has grown cold over the years because the love was not nourished. This causes much pain and heartache. But Christ is the restorer (Joel 2:25), and He will pour out His Spirit upon us (Joel 2:29). He alone is the healer of our hearts.

In Revelation, John writes of a love that has become lukewarm.

"So then because thou art lukewarm, and neither cold nor hot, I will spue thee out of my mouth" (Rev. 3:16).

This is a warning and a prophetic utterance.

The bridegroom, Jesus Christ, desires a lover who is passionate for Him.

If your love for Him has grown cold or, worse, lukewarm, turn back to Him. Do an about-face—a complete 180-degree turn around going to the opposite direction.

Lukewarm food has no taste. It is not pleasing to eat. One would select hot soup or cold soup, French onion soup or vichyssoise (cold potato soup). Both are extremely delicious when served at the correct temperature. But lukewarm food is not appetizing.

When we have no feelings for Him, He also finds us to be lukewarm and tasteless.[19]

Passionate love is exactly what the Song of Songs is about. May the Holy Spirit lead you into a greater depth in your relationship with Jesus as you study and learn the depth, within the Song of Songs, of His love for you, His bride.

---

[19]   Gwen R. Schmidt, *The Marriage Song* (Singapore: Creative Service, 1962), 9.

> Kisses involve loving action. Kisses are personalized and sweet.
>
> To be lovingly kissed by your Bridegroom is proof that two hearts did meet!
>
> Lord, help us to be aware of the many tokens of Your love to us today.
>
> Help us to accept the intimacy that flows from Your hand many ways.
>
>

3 Because of the savour of thy good ointments thy name is as ointment poured forth, therefore do the virgins love thee.

> *"Thy name* is as ointment poured forth" (Song 1:3b). [Emphasis added]

> "I will set him on high, because he hath known *my name"* (Ps. 91:14b). [Emphasis added]

> *"The name* of the Lord is a strong tower: the righteous runneth into it, and is safe" (Prov. 18:10). [Emphasis added]

> "I am the Lord: that is *my name*: and my glory will I not give to another" (Isa. 42:8a).

"Wherefore God also hath highly exalted him and *given him a name* which is above every name: That at the name of Jesus every knee should bow, of things in heaven, and things in earth, and things under the earth: And that every tongue should confess that Jesus Christ is Lord to the glory of God the Father" (Phil. 2:9–11). [Emphasis added]

> Jesus, Jesus, Jesus. There's just something about that name.
> Savior, Master, Jesus, like the fragrance after the rain.
> Jesus, Jesus, Jesus, Let all heaven and earth proclaim,
> Kings and kingdoms may all pass away,
> But there's something about that name. (Gloria Gaither)

Ointment speaks of a good old-fashioned healing balm. Ointment applied to a wound brings healing.

The mighty name of Jesus has been given to us, and we have this "power of attorney" to apply His name to every situation of healing that is needed.

Jesus blood was poured out on Calvary. His death on the cross was so that many could experience the fragrance of His life and His love worldwide.

It cost Him everything to lay down His life, and the fragrance of this healing gift is everlasting.

"...therefore do the virgins love thee" (Song 1:3c).

The virgins are the separated ones, the holy ones who know *His name* and know how to apply His name to every situation life brings.

They are in love with Him. They know that the very mention of *His name* brings health, joy, love, and peace.

In Matthew 25, the parable of the virgins tells of five virgins who have sufficient oil and five virgins who have run out of oil. Truly, this oil is a representation of the Holy Spirit. We need to be filled with the Holy Spirit. To be filled with Him will affect everything we do. We will speak *His name*, for Jesus' name heals, delivers, and sets free.

> Lord, I desire to be refilled with Your Spirit. I know it will affect all I do.
>
> Help me to walk in Your Spirit until Your Spirit controls my life view.
>
> When I am filled with Your Spirit. When I set time aside for only You.
>
> Then with confident authority, folk will be healed, delivered and renewed.
>
> It is a privilege to be filled with Your Spirit. It is a result of time alone with You.
>
> Keep me so intimately focused on You, that my mind will know Your point of view.
>
>

4   Draw me, we will run after thee: the king hath brought me into his chambers: we will be glad and rejoice in thee, we will remember thy love more than wine: the upright love thee.

In tender love, He draws us to Himself. He gently pulls us to Himself.

When we quiet ourselves from the busyness of the day, we can feel His love drawing us. He pulls us up out of the miry clay of circumstances and to Himself. Whenever we go through difficulties, He is there to draw us to Himself. Even in joyful, peaceful times, He is there to draw us to Himself.

"No man can come to me, except the Father which hath sent me draw him" (John 6:44a).

When we are drawn to Him we run towards Him and He brings us into His secret secluded place within His dwelling place – the dwelling place of the king.

"He that dwelleth in the secret place of the most High shall abide under the shadow of the Almighty" (Ps. 91:1).

There is a place in God, a secret place, a chamber inside, a bedroom, a sanctuary, an inner room such as the Holy of Holies, a secluded portion of the palace, where we desire to be with Him.

A chorus of the daughters of Jerusalem

"...we will be glad and rejoice in thee" (Song 1:4b).

Enter into the secret chamber with Him and rejoice in Him.

"Because thou hast made the LORD, which is my refuge, even the most High, thy habitation" (Ps. 91:9).

Your habitation is in Him. Your secret place is in Him. Your place in God is in His chamber. It is there we will remember His love. We review, rehearse, and ponder on His great love. We count our blessings. We rejoice.

"We will remember thy love more than wine" (Song 1:4c).

The love of the Lord is the best love. It never fades. It is consistent. His love for His bride is so great that He laid down His life as a sacrifice for our sin that we might be righteous before God.

His love gave all; His love is perfect. Always remember His love. He desires your love in return.

"...love the Lord thy God with all thy heart, and with all thy soul, and with all thy mind, and with all thy strength: this is the first commandment" (Mark 12:30).

"...the upright love thee" (Song 1:4d).

This is a distinguished group of people—an honorable people. Here are some of the promises of the upright.

> "Surely the righteous shall give thanks unto thy name: the upright shall dwell in thy presence" (Ps. 140:13).

> "For the upright shall dwell in the land, and the perfect shall remain in it" (Prov. 2:21).

> "The righteousness of the upright shall deliver them: but transgressors shall be taken in their own naughtiness" (Prov. 11:6).

> "The words of the wicked are to lie in wait for blood: but the mouth of the upright shall deliver them" (Prov. 12:6).

> "Righteousness keepeth him that is upright in the way: but wickedness overthroweth the sinner" (Prov. 13:6).

The bride knows and understands that others love Him too.

The Shulamite and the Shepherd King

5   I am black, but comely, O ye daughters of Jerusalem, as the tents of Kedar, as the curtains of Solomon.

The Shulamite says, "I am black." The Shepherd King says, "But comely, O ye daughters of Jerusalem." The Shulamite says, "As the tents of Kedar." The Shepherd King says, "as the curtain of Solomon."

"I am black," (Song 1:5a).

The Shulamite has been working in the fields, under the sun. She knew her skin was darkened from working in the fields, and she feels that she stands out from other women.

The Shepherd King replies, "…but comely" (Song 1:5b).

She may appear as an outcast to others, but He sees her as comely—pleasant to look at and beautiful in His eyes.

The Shulamite continues, "as the tents of Kedar" (Song 1:5c).

The tents of Kedar belonged to Ishmael's second son.

"And these are the names of the sons of Ishmael, by their names, according to their generations: the firstborn of Ishmael, Nebajoth; and Kedar, and Adbeel, and Mibsam" (Gen. 25:13).

The tents of Kedar are similar to the Bedouin Arabs today who dwell in tents that are made of goat's hair.[20]

Ishmael was not the son included in the covenant that God established with Isaac, but Ishamel was blessed too.

The Shulamite compares herself to the Gentiles' tents and not to the children of Abraham, but the king compares her to the curtains of Solomon.

The church too is "black" in original sin and transgression with many spots and infirmities. "The effect of sin has been to destroy in the human heart the love of God, and substitute for it the love of unworthy things."[21] But Glory to God, through the imputation of His righteousness, the church becomes beautiful.

"...as the curtains of Solomon" (Song 1:5d).

The hangings of tapestry in Solomon's palace were costly and magnificent. "The curtains of Solomon" means the hangings and veil of Solomon's temple, typifying Christ's righteousness.[22]

"Know ye not that ye are the temple of God, and that the Spirit of God dwelleth in you?" (1 Cor. 3:16).

---

[20] Carl Friedrich Keil and Franz Delitzsch, *Commentary on the Old Testament: New Updated Edition*, Electronic Database, (Peabody, MA: Hendrickson, 1996), Song of Solomon.

[21] George A. Burrowes, *Commentary on the Song of Solomon*. (Carlisle, Pennsylvania: The Banner of Truth Trust, 1853), 9.

[22] Andrew Robert Fausset, *Fausset's Bible Dictionary, Jamieson, Fausset, and Brown Commentary*. (Electronic Database by Biblesoft, Inc., 1997), Song of Solomon.

> If the Spirit of God dwells in me, then my life must be free from all sin.
>
> Lord, purify me daily and completely so that Your Spirit feels welcome within.
>
>

The Shulamite

6 Look not upon me, because I am black, because the sun hath looked upon me: my mother's children were angry with me; they made me the keeper of the vineyards; but mine own vineyard have I not kept.

She has been forced to work, labor, and toil in the hot sun, and her skin has become darkened by the sun. Her brothers and sisters gave this job to her. Their anger is a sign of their preference for themselves. Yet God sees her in the field. Just as God saw the people of Israel toiling under the hand of pharaoh and just as God sees you toiling, He sees the Shulamite. Her deliverance comes at the place she suffers most.

Our Lord Jesus Christ walked by us one day and saw us toiling under the load of sin. "He saw in us something He could use. He saw in us something that we didn't see in ourselves."[23]

---

[23] Gwen R. Schmidt, *The Marriage Song.* (Singapore: Creative Service, 1962), 16.

He called us to Himself. Once we were blackened by sin, but the blood of Jesus makes us white as snow.

The bride here is introduced proclaiming her own weakness. Here, as we consider this as a divine poem, expressing the mutual love between Christ and his church, "it agrees very well with the other parts of the sacred writings, wherein the infirmities of God's own people are not concealed; not even of those who were themselves the penmen of them; which is a strong proof of their divine authority."[24]

Lord, You know my deep-seated weaknesses. Yet You love me in spite of them all.

Help me to remember Whose I am and that forgiveness at Calvary still covers it all.

You see me as Your Beloved Lovable Bride. You see me as someone You could use.

Forgiving me for not enjoying Your Love. May You use my talents to carry Good News.

7 Tell me, O thou whom my soul loveth, where thou feedest, where thou makest thy flock to rest at noon: for why should I be as one that turneth aside by the flocks of thy companions?

---

[24] John Gill, *An Exposition of the Song of Solomon*. (Grand Rapids, Michigan: Sovereign Grace Publishers, 1971), 2.

The Shulamite is deeply in love with her Lord. Her very soul is possessed by this great love. It is this deep love that carries her, the bride of Christ, through every day of her life until she crosses the great divide and is with Him in eternity.

Mike Bickle of International House of Prayer, Kansas City, illustrated Mark 12:30, "Thou shalt love the Lord thy God with all thy heart, with all thy soul, and with all thy mind, and with all thy strength." This is the first and greatest commandment. He proclaimed, "This love for our Lord will spill over into our relationships with others. If we love Him completely we will love others completely. This love must be given priority, for it is the most important of all the commandments of God."[25]

"...where thou feedest, where thou makest thy flock to rest at noon" (Song 1:7a).

Noon is when the sun is directly overhead, and it can be the hottest part of the day. The Shulamite wants to come aside with her beloved under the shade of the trees. There she will rest with her Lord before returning to her flock and their needs.

In ministry, it is vital that one has a daily time alone with our Lord. In service and work of any kind, a daily time of prayer and the Word and thoughtful contemplation are needed. Have you ever not made time for the Lord and then come to the conclusion that your day would have been better if you had only set

---

[25] Mike Bickle, "Loving Jesus: The First Commandment Established in First Place" (sermon delivered at New Life Church, Virginia Beach, VA, July 2016.)

aside your tasks to spend time with Him? Has He truly captured your heart? Do your tasks capture your heart more than Him? Is your life too busy for Him? Turn, change your mind today, and schedule Him into your daily life—You will find rest for your soul.

> ...for why should I be as one that turneth aside by the flocks of thy companions? (Song 1:7b)

There were other shepherd girls keeping sheep or goats, but she sought after the Lord. She was lonely in the field every day, but she set her heart and mind to *seek after only the Lord*. She would take no substitute.

The Shepherd King

8 If thou know not, O thou fairest among women, go thy way forth by the footsteps of the flock, and feed thy kids beside the shepherds' tents.

"O thou fairest among women" (Song 1:8a).

He has set His eyes on me, and He tells me that I am the most beautiful among women. He loves me!

There is no one else that draws His attention. We are His bride, and He has set His love on us. As we prepare for the wedding, "the glory of the Lord is risen upon [us]" (Isaiah 60:1). We radiate His love to Him and to others.

The glory of the Lord is seen upon us, and Gentiles will come to our light.

> "If thou know not... go thy way forth by the footsteps of the flock" (Song 1:8a, c).

Go ahead. Get moving and find Him. Don't just sit around. Get up and get moving.

You can tell where He is because the sheep have left their footprints in the field. This is where we will find Him. There will be the signs of others seeking Him too. "For where two or three are gathered together in my name, there am I in the midst of them" (Matt. 18:20). We will follow wherever He leads. Let us remember to not forsake "the assembling of ourselves together... [as the day of the Lord draws near]" (Heb. 10:25).

> "...and feed thy kids beside the shepherds' tents" (Song 1:8d).

Shepherd King is near His tents, in the place near the sanctuary of His tents. There, you can bring your burdens to Him. There, you will find rest for your soul. There, you will find food and sustenance for thy kids (those within your care), beside the Shepherd's tents.

> Lord, You've brought some wounded souls into my life.
>
> You know their personal, sensitive, deep needs.
>
> Help me to tarry long enough in Your Presence, Lord
>
> That wisdom from Yourself will help them plant seeds.

9 I have compared thee, O my love, to a company of horses in Pharaoh's chariots.

To be compared to a royal steed, one of pharaoh's finest horses, is a love language of ancient times. The horses that pulled the pharaoh's chariots were strong, stately, swift, and spirited. Egypt had the best horses.

Solomon also had war horses. These were not lazy horses. These were not the Sunday afternoon "Let's go for a ride" horses. These horses were ready for battle.

"And Solomon had forty thousand stalls of horses for His chariots, and twelve thousand horsemen" (1 Kings 4:26).

Let's consider the horse written about in Job.

Hast thou given the horse strength? hast thou clothed his neck with thunder? Canst thou make him afraid as a grasshopper? the glory of his nostrils is terrible. He paweth in the valley, and rejoiceth in his strength: he goeth on to meet the armed men. He mocketh at fear, and is not affrighted; neither turneth he back from the sword. The quiver rattleth against him, the glittering spear and the shield. He swalloweth the ground with fierceness and rage: neither believeth he that it is the sound of the trumpet. He saith among the trumpets, Ha, ha; and he smelleth the battle afar off, the thunder of the captains, and the shouting (Job 39:19–25).

Solomon compares the Shulamite to this type of steed. To say she is merely "spirited" is not sufficient.

The horse spoken of in Job is strong with its neck clothed with thunder, who paws at the ground and is ready for battle, mocks at fear, swallows the ground with fierceness and rage, and runs at the sound of the trumpet.

So, to be compared to a horse—a fine steed of the best of pharaoh's chariots—is highly complementary.

When we hear the sound of the trumpet, we too should be ready for war. And we will run at the sound of the trumpet, saying, "Ha, ha."

Matthew Henry says, "We are weak in ourselves, but if Christ makes us as horses, strong and bold, we need not fear what all the powers of darkness can do against us."[26]

10 Thy cheeks are comely with rows of jewels, thy neck with chains of gold.

He admires the ornaments of her countenance. With what ornaments have you been graced?

He admires the beauty and ornaments of her countenance. The ornaments are disposed in rows and chains, and Henry says this represents that "there is a mutual connection with dependence on each other,"[27] similar to other saints in the Body of Christ.

The bride has prepared herself with ornaments and jewels. She has made herself ready.

Isaiah writes of the blessedness of the church. "I will greatly rejoice in the Lord, my soul shall be joyful in my God: for he hath clothed me with the garments of salvation, he hath covered me with the robe of righteousness, as a bridegroom decketh himself with ornaments, as a bride adorneth herself with jewels" (Isa. 61:10).

The rows of jewels and chains of gold are made in preparation for the wedding. The jewels of gold and silver are gifts of

---

26   Matthew Henry, *Matthew Henry's Commentary on the Whole Bible: New Modern Edition*, (Electronic Database by Biblesoft, Inc.: Hendrickson Publishers, Inc., 1991), Song of Solomon.

27   Ibid.

the bridegroom to His bride. A poor shepherd girl would not have had the ability to purchase such expensive jewels—chains of gold and silver. Truly, the Lord has marked His bride with gifts that set her apart from the rest of the world. We are marked with redemption. We show forth the beauty of the bride.

The chains of gold may also represent the fear of the Lord.

> "The fear of the *Lord* is the beginning of knowledge: but fools despise wisdom and instruction. My son, hear the instruction of thy father, and forsake not the law of thy mother: For they shall be an ornament of grace unto thy head, and chains about thy neck" (Prov. 1:7–9).

11 We will make thee borders of gold with studs of silver.

Silver in the scripture points to redemption, the price paid to Judas Iscariot (Matt. 26:15).

We are redeemed from our sins because of the precious blood of Christ. We, His bride, receive the gold and silver representing the deity of Christ.

The Shulamite

12 While the king sitteth at his table, my spikenard sendeth forth the smell thereof.

Another scripture that mentions *spikenard* is in Mark 14:3 that tells of the woman with the alabaster box who poured the spikenard on Jesus' head.

Read verse 13 below and consider the implications.

13 A bundle of myrrh is my well beloved unto me; he shall lie all night betwixt my breasts.

The Song of Solomon gives us a multitude of pictures that foreshadow Jesus Christ and His saving grace.

The suffering of Jesus on the cross is represented here as a tied bundle of myrrh over her heart. This tied up bundle of myrrh is an incredible picture of the cross of Jesus Christ. Myrrh was one of the gifts of the Magi, a sign that Jesus would suffer. Myrrh is an embalming spice.

Here in this verse, the bride wears a bundle of myrrh tied near her heart, representative of the fragrance of His suffering. She carries on her chest the fragrance of Him but she is not sorrowful. Myrrh is an outer anointing.

There is an inner anointing as well. Although not spoken of here, it is important to note that in addition to the bundle of myrrh over her heart, signifying suffering, she also carries the fragrance of Jesus' anointing.

The prophet says, "God, thy God, hath anointed thee [Jesus] with the oil of gladness above thy fellows," (Ps. 45:7) and Peter says that Jesus was anointed with the Spirit, "How God anointed Jesus of Nazareth with the Holy Ghost" (Acts

10:38). This ointment of Christ is the Holy Spirit and is called the oil of gladness, and is a "joining together of many graces giving a sweet fragrance." "Gladness does not anoint the body but brightens the inmost heart."[28]

The fragrance of Jesus Christ is the fragrance of suffering and the oil of gladness. The myrrh represents Jesus' suffering, and the Holy Spirit's fragrance upon Jesus is the oil of gladness.

And this is the fragrance we carry of Him wherever we go. "For we are unto God a sweet savour of Christ" (2 Cor. 2:15).

Her thoughts of Him refresh her like the most fragrant flowers.

> Lord, You want to fill us with Your Fragrance.
> Your Presence offers aromas of Peace.
> Help us to wait long enough in Your Presence
> Until Your Divine Refreshing offers release.
>
> Lord, the fragrance of You rests upon me.
> I am privileged to represent Your Love.
> May I remain long enough in Your Presence
> That I carry Your perfume from above.
>
>

---

[28] Saint Ambrose of Milan, *De Fide and De Spiritu Sancto,* (Morrisville, NC: Pilgrimage House Press, 2010), 285, 286.

14 My beloved is unto me as a cluster of camphire in the vineyards of Engedi.

Engedi ("ain-Jidy" the fountain of the kid, of the lamb) is a place 400 feet above the west shore of the Dead Sea, where there are fountains of warm water that flow out from beneath the limestone cliffs and cascade down to a fertile plain half a mile broad and a mile in length. Here in ancient times, there were vineyards of palms and sugar cane and melons. Camphire and balsam and edible fruits grew there. This was one of the world's famed garden spots.[29]

This beautiful garden was built by Solomon. He developed the great gardens with a fountain in the center amidst the wilderness. The bride says that her beloved is like a garden where she can be refreshed.

Here, *camphire* translates to *henna*, and the word in Hebrew is כפר (koper) and is scientifically known as *Lawsonia inermis*.

This flowering shrub not only has tiny white blossoms but also grows with pink and yellow blossoms.

Interestingly, the Hebrew word is a homonym. The word *koper* also means redemption paid, to buy out, redeem, or to be ransomed.[30]

---

[29] Thompson Chain-Reference Bible, (Indianapolis, IN: Kirkbride Bible Co., 1998), Engedi.
[30] The Strongest Strong's Exhaustive Concordance of the Bible, (Grand Rapids, Michigan: Zondervan Publishing Company, 2001), koper.

The Shepherd King

15 Behold, thou art fair, my love; behold, thou art fair; thou hast doves' eyes.

Two times he has told His bride, "Behold thou art fair." He calls her "my love," "thou hast doves' eyes." The physical feature that is described here is "thou hast dove's eyes." He does not say, "Thou hast eyes of a hawk, like a tyrant."

This candid comment is to make a point—The nature of a dove is gentle, trusting, and sweet. The nature of a hawk is never gentle, trusting, and sweet. A hawk is out for "the kill." To have the eyes of a dove is symbolical and representative of the presence of the Holy Spirit within the life of the bride. She is calm. Her eyes are meek, gentle, trusting, and sweet. Her eyes are innocent.

The bride communicates her love to the king through the action of her eyes that depict her heart—her thoughts for Him, her desire for Him, and her love for Him.

> "Charity suffereth long, and is kind; charity envieth not; charity vaunteth not itself, is not puffed up, Doth not behave itself unseemly, seeketh not her own, is not easily provoked, thinketh no evil; Rejoiceth not in iniquity, but rejoiceth in the truth; Beareth all things, believeth all things, hopeth all things, endureth all things" (1 Cor. 13:4–7).

She trusts Him explicitly.

> May the Lord cause my eyes to be so filled with kindness
> That lonely folk will be drawn to Your Love.
> May even my glance in their direction
> Remind them that a loving God is above.
>
> May I encourage them to trust You completely.
> May the Love of the Lord shine clearly through.
> So that whatever words are spoken in their presence
> Will become a gracious representation of You.

The Shulamite

16 Behold, thou art fair, my beloved, yea, pleasant: also our bed is green.

17 The beams of our house are cedar, and our rafters of fir.

This is her reply. She calls Him "my beloved." She echoes His heart.

The "cedar" and "fir" were used in the temple (1 Kings 5:6–10). The fir is hard, durable, and fragrant. The cedar is hard and fragrant. It is a place for communion between God and man.

"The green of the bed is similar to a green oasis in the desert."[31] Or it could be a summer house. Green is very refreshing to the eyes.

Fragrant cedar is used today in closets and hope chests to protect fabric and fur. Cedar shakes are a siding for the interior or exterior of a home and contain natural oils.

> When cedar trees are planted in Israel, growth and fragrance soon take place.
>
> Tree planting is considering the future. Healthy trees refurbish God's space.
>
> Lord, may we represent growing cedars? May we offer protection to flourish for You.
>
> When healthy, natural growth becomes obvious, the Presence of God will shine through.
>
>

---

[31] Andrew Robert Fausset, *Fausset's Bible Dictionary.* (Electronic Database by Biblesoft, Inc., 1997), Song of Solomon.

Notes

Chapter 2

The Shulamite

1   I am the rose of Sharon, and the lily of the valleys.

According to Barnes, there are two different interpretations for this verse. "The majority of Christian fathers assigned this verse to Christ the King. Hebrew commentators assign this verse to the bride." [32] Henry asserts that,

> Jesus Christ, Son of God, the bright and morning star, is known as the rose of Sharon and the lily of the valleys. He is accessible and there is beauty and sweetness in him. Christ is the rose of the field and that tells us that the gospel is common salvation. It is available to all. He is not a rose locked away in a garden but all may come to him. [33]

The lily is white and sweet and in the low places.

Here in Song 2:1, I agree with the Hebrew commentators and believe it is the Shulamite who is speaking. (A clearer understanding is provided when we read Song 2:2.)

---

[32]   Albert Barnes, *Barnes' Notes*, (Electronic Database by Biblesoft, Inc., 1997), Song of Solomon.

[33]   Matthew Henry, *Matthew Henry's Commentary on the Whole Bible: New Modern Edition*, (Electronic Database by Biblesoft, Inc.: Hendrickson Publishers, Inc., 1996), Song of Solomon.

She desires to be like Him. We have His example. He is perfect; and we desire, with the help of the Holy Spirit, to be more like Him each and every day—beautiful sweet, lowly (not arrogant), humble, delicate, and modest. These are the qualities of these humble wild flowers.

The Shulamite is comparing herself to a meadow flower. This might possibly be a crocus flower—a rose of the field—or a narcissus (daffodil), a wild flower.

She is well aware of her rural simplicity and lowliness, yet she does not speak of herself in a derogatory manner.

(Note: Sharon has two locations. Sharon is a Mediterranean coastal plain between Joppa and Syria and also a location between Mount Tabor and the Sea of Tiberius, which would be near the bride's home, if she were from Shunem.)

2 As the lily among thorns, so is my love among the daughters.

The Shulamite is the lily among thorns, and none can compare to her grace and beauty. She excels in grace and beauty more than her companions.

Luther examines these two verses and determines that the Shulamite is the lily, the rose of Christ. Luther writes, "If thou art the lily and the rose of Christ, know that thy dwelling place is among thorns. Only take heed, lest by impatience, rash judgments, and pride, thou thyself become a thorn."[34]

---

[34] Martin Luther, *History of the Great Reformation of the Sixteenth Century in Germany, Switzerland & C.*, Trans. J. H. Merle D'Aubigne. (New York: Robert

Thorns are wicked, unprofitable, and hurtful to others. We, the bride, are His darling companion, and we stand out from all the rest.

The thorns are the curse of sin (Gen. 3:18). We do not fight against the thorns, but we bear them patiently.

Often, we want to complain that we are a lily among thorns and that we have been planted in the wrong place. But as our Heavenly Father looks down on us from on high, He can spot us immediately. We stand out from all the rest.

> Even the pure white, lowly lily is designed to flourish and spread.
>
> Lord help us to be like the lily and become fragrant where'er we are led.
>
> Lowliness does not mean to be discarded. Humility can be a restful place.
>
> Lowly lilies create a beautiful carpet. In God's garden, no plant is a waste!
>
> Maybe a lost sinner will find the Lord. Perhaps a crusty Christian could be healed.
>
> Thorny places create masterpieces for the Lord. His creativity is already sealed.
>
>

Carter, 1846), 188.

3 As the apple tree among the trees of the wood, so is my beloved among the sons. I sat down under His shadow with great delight, and His fruit was sweet to my taste.

Jesus Christ is the one tree that stands out from all the rest. The fragrance of this apple tree is like no other tree in the wood.

The Shulamite is delighted to find this one and only apple tree, and she plucks off one large, crisp apple and takes a bite. The fruit is succulent, juicy and sweet. It is not a sour or green apple, but it is a fresh ripe apple. There, she sits down and rests—right under the fruit tree. Are you willing to sit and rest under His shadow?

"He who dwells in the secret place of the most High God shall abide under the shadow of the Almighty" (Ps. 91:1).

> Sitting and waiting in my Beloved's Arms is the best place of all to be.
> There are secrets revealed to no one else. Intimacy with Him sets us free.
>
>

4 He brought me to the banqueting house, and His banner over me was love.

A banner is some type of sign elevated on a pole. Here, it is the emblem of the king. It is a sign of His authority.

"We will rejoice in thy salvation, and in the name of our God we will set up our banners: the Lord fulfill all thy petitions" (Ps. 20:5).

"Thou has given a banner to them that fear thee, that it may be displayed because of the truth" (Ps. 60:4).

And Moses built an altar, and called the name of it "Jehovah-Nissi" [The Lord is my banner] (Exod. 17:15).

His love is her banner. A banner is a flag, like a pennant, sometimes bearing a symbol or a logo, or a message or a slogan, or a coat of arms.

The banqueting house is translated as the house of wine.

> Banners are signs of authority.
> Banners are meant to be displayed.
> Your Beloved placed a Banner over you.
> With His Love, Your future is laid.
>
> So bask in the blessings of His Banner.
> Hold confidently to the privileges it brings.
> His Banner over you is unique.
> His Banner declares you Beloved of the King.
>
>

5 Stay me with flagons, comfort me with apples: for I am sick of love.

Flagons are dried grape (raisin) cakes, or date cakes, or fig cakes (2 Sam. 6:19) (1 Chron. 16:3) (1 Sam. 30:12).

There is a reviving power in the fruit, and the Shulamite needs refreshing because she is lovesick. She desires bodily refreshment. She desires tokens of His affection.

> If you stop long enough to listen,
> If you stop long enough to contemplate,
> You'll be amazed at all His Love Gifts.
> Your refreshing from Him is never late.
>
>

6 His left hand is under my head, and his right hand doth embrace me.

Jesus's arms and hands of love embrace you. Do not be afraid.

This reminds me of a beautiful song by Paul Wilbur, *Dance with Me*.

> Dance with me Oh Lover of my soul, to the song of all songs,

Romance me Oh Lover of my soul, to the song of all songs,
Behold you have come over the hills upon the mountain,
To Me you have run, My Beloved, You've captured my heart.

Dance with me Oh Lover of my soul, to the song of all songs,
Romance me Oh Lover of my soul, to the song of all songs,
With you, I will go You are my Love You are my fair One,
The winter has passed and the springtime has come.

He embraces me. He embraces you, so gently, so lovingly, so tenderly. Let Him hold you.

"Casting all your care on him; for he careth for you" (1 Pet. 5:7).

Here in His embrace, we are comforted. And we rest. No harm can come to us when we are protected by His loving embrace.

Let go of the other things in your life that do not truly satisfy your soul and rest in His embrace.

> Imagine the feeling of His Presence as He caresses your head in His hands!
> Imagine His Embrace and His Comfort! His Protection is strong and it stands!
>
>

7 I charge you, O ye daughters of Jerusalem, by the roes, and by the hinds of the field, that ye stir not up, nor awake my love, till he please.

This charge is a command the bride gives so that others do not come and break her intimate time with her Lord. Do you protect your intimate time with Him, or is it interrupted by a telephone call, a Facebook message, or a *pling*, notifying you of a text message?

When I taught homeschool, I let voice mail answer every telephone call during the school day. Nothing was permitted to break the continuity of instruction, and I guarded this time well. Protecting school time permitted me to successfully complete the scope and sequence of lessons each day.

Our time with Jesus must be protected and guarded, too. You are His bride. So too, the Shulamite commands others, by all that is swift and gentle, to not awaken or disturb her Lord. Protect, guard, and keep your intimate time with Him. Be swift and yet gentle to protect your time with Him.

Prioritize your time with Your Beloved. Clear your calendar a few days ahead.

Intimate time with Your Lover offers the intimacy of His Presence as you are led.

8 The voice of my beloved! behold, he cometh leaping upon the mountains, skipping upon the hills.

Delitzsch's perspective is:

> The locality is no longer the royal city. The Shulamite is at home. Her home stands among the rocks, deep in the mountain range; around are the vineyards which the family have planted, and hill-pastures on which they feed their flocks. She looks longingly for her distant lover.[35]

His voice will be heard on that joyful day when he comes to gather His bride. He is leaping and skipping. He is joyful as He comes to call us home. Our ears are tuned and waiting to hear only His voice. No other voice moves us the way His voice moves us.

I feel such joy and thankfulness as I read this scripture. I praise Him for saving a sinner like me. Thank you Jesus for

---

[35] Carl Friedrich Keil and Franz Delitzsch, *Commentary on the Old Testament: New Updated Edition*, Electronic Database, (Peabody, MA: Hendrickson, 1996), Song of Solomon.

dying and shedding your blood on the cross at Calvary. After three days, You resurrected from the grave. Before You departed for heaven You told us that You would come again. I wait with the anticipation for the day of Your return.

Listen, can you hear the sound of His footsteps?

> The sounds of the footsteps of Jesus are anticipated with joy in my heart.
>
> My Bridegroom is coming to claim me, then we'll never again be apart.
>
> I am so privileged to be numbered among His Church, His Bride to be!
>
> Lord, thank You for choosing to love me. Your coming will bring ecstasy for me!
>
>

9   My beloved is like a roe or a young hart: behold, he standeth behind our wall, he looketh forth at the windows, shewing himself through the lattice.

A roe or a young hart moves swiftly and gently. Suddenly, He will appear at your side.

Here in verse 9, he is just beyond the wall, "showing himself through the lattice." He comes close by, and He watches us. At times, we catch a glimpse of Him. This time, He is coming to speak to you, to call you to Himself. Listen.

The Shulamite

10 My beloved spake, and said unto me, Rise up, my love, my
fair one, and come away.

Are you in time and rhythm to hear His voice? Are you
listening? His voice speaks. We can miss His voice if we are not
listening. Are you too busy with things, and the cares of this
world, to set aside time to listen for His voice? He is speaking
to you now.

"Rise up" (Song 2:10b). That is an action on your part and
on my part.

We must listen first and then arise. He wants us to move at
His command. He calls us gently; He calls us "My love," "My
fair one." He desires that we "come away."

A listening ear and a heart sensitive to the timing of the
Holy Spirit is vital to the bride. If we rise before He commands,
then we move in our own timing, our own rhythm. Wait on the
Lord. When He speaks, arise. He has much work for you to do
in the Kingdom, but wait for His leading. It will come.

Listen. Arise.

> Listening for His Voice is a privilege. Everyone is *not* automatically in tune.
>
> Lord, keep my ears alert and listening. Your coming for Your Bride could be soon.
>
> Help me to wait for Your Leading. Help me to always recognize Your Voice.
>
> I want to be alert to Your Moving. I want to be obedient, my first choice!
>
>

The Bridegroom King

11 For, lo, the winter is past, the rain is over and gone.

If you have ever lived north of Richmond, Virginia, or north of St. Louis, Missouri, you have probably experienced a snowfall in the winter months. In the northern United States and in Canada, snowfall is beautiful in the winter, but it can be quite treacherous. Heating your home is expensive. Traveling is sometimes very difficult, and there can be days when you might get snowed in and unable to travel anywhere because the roads are not plowed. And when the roads are plowed, sand is often applied so that drivers in their vehicles will not slip off the road. Winter can be difficult and cold.

And then, one morning, you awaken, the snow has melted, the rains have stopped, and there is the sound of birds chirping. Look! The winter is past. The rain is over and gone.

Sometimes in our lives, times of testing and trials are like going through winter. We wait. We pray, "When will this be over?" We trust Him.

The bridegroom calls you to arise (Song 2:10) for Spring is in the air. Winter is over and past. The rain is over and gone.

> Lord, You've allowed frigid winter to come upon us.
> You've shown us barren dormancy without seed.
> But *now* the promise of Spring is all ready
> Winter's depression will become a memory unseen!
>
> Thank You for the Promise of Springtime.
> Thank You for all life's seasons that change.
> The warmth of our Beloved always blesses us
> With new life through Your Spirit—we're rearranged!
>
>

12 The flowers appear on the earth; the time of the singing of birds is come, and the voice of the turtle is heard in our land.

Winter is over. Springtime has arrived. Spring is the season of life. Winter is the season of death when the seed that has fallen to the ground dies so it can grow again. In spring, everywhere you see and hear life.

Spring is a picture of joy. Flowers appear on earth, the birds sing, and the turtle [dove] is heard. Life begins again.

In, *Surprised by Joy*, C. S. Lewis explains that in his early years, joy eluded him. He had experienced only "arrows of joy" since childhood. There had never been the slightest hint "that there ever had been or ever would be any connection between God and joy." [36]

Life begins again for C. S. Lewis when he makes the leap from atheism to theism and then from theism to Christianity, he experiences joy.

Do you have this "joy unspeakable and full of glory" (1 Pet. 1:8) in your relationship with Christ Jesus our Lord? Lewis writes, "Joy is the serious business of heaven." [37]

Do you feel the joy that comes with springtime?

If joy has been alluding you, your winter is over, Spring is here. This invitation is for you to experience joy again!

---

[36]   C. S. Lewis, *Surprised by Joy: The Shape of My Early Life* (New York, NY: Harper Collins Publishers, 2017) 281.
[37]   C. S. Lewis, Letters to Malcolm: Chiefly on Prayer, (San Diego, CA: Harvest House Publishing, 1964) 92, 93.

Lord, return to my heart the joy of Springtime.
Renew those God-given emotions once more.
When the love of my Bridegroom is upon me.
Relationship with Him renews and even soars!

13 The fig tree putteth forth her green figs, and the vines with the tender grape give a good smell. Arise, my love, my fair one, and come away.

The fig tree blooming is the sign of spring. The fragrance of the grapes permeates the air. Again He calls, "Arise, my love, my fair one, and come away." His voice is as refreshing as the scenery—the birds singing, the flowers blossoming, the fig tree putting forth its fruit, and the tender fragrance of the grapes.

His voice calls to His bride to arise and come away, now that the winter is past and Spring has arrived. Listen. You can hear His voice.

Listen for the voice of your Bridegroom.
His loving call is for you today.
His voice magnifies His Love for you.
As you listen simply trust and obey.

Obey as you're making final preparations.
Obey as you invite other souls to come.
Behold your Beloved Bridegroom cometh.
Is that His music I hear with a hum?

14 O my dove, that art in the clefts of the rock, in the secret places of the stairs, let me see thy countenance, let me hear thy voice; for sweet is thy voice, and thy countenance is comely.

He calls us "my dove." The dove is gentle and sweet, pure, and innocent. Here, "my dove" is an expression of endearment. The dove typifies the change in one that is converted.[38]

Here, it describes how after one is converted, their sinful state disappears. They appear honorable. "Though ye have lien among the pots, yet shall ye be as the wings of a dove covered with silver, and her feathers with yellow gold" (Ps. 68:13).

---

38 Robert Jamieson, A.R. Fausset & David Brown, *Jamieson, Fausset and Brown Commentary*, (Electronic Database by Biblesoft, Inc., 1997), Song of Solomon.

The dove is hiding, resting, and tucked away within the clefts of the rock. He urges us to come forth from our rock home. He wants to see our face. He desires to hear our voice.

We are His people and His bride. He tells us that we are "comely."

Lift your face and your voice to Him and tell Him that He is lovely. Thank Him for how He has kept you from year to year. Thank Him for watching over you.

> Lord, Thank You for Your daily Precious Promises
> That have offered personalized, secure love to me.
> At times I am so timid and vulnerable
> But Your loving Protection is available to see.
>
>

15 Take us the foxes, the little foxes, that spoil the vines: for our vines have tender grapes.

"Take us." This is something that we will do together with Him, praise God! He warns of foxes—little foxes that spoil the vines. Foxes are crafty and sly, swift creatures that will eat at the vine and the tender grapes. The foxes will come. We have been warned, but He will help us. The foxes come when our vines have tender grapes. The vineyard is a picture of our relationship with the king. Let us jealously guard our love for Him and defend our relationship with Him.

> These foxes point to all the great and little enemies and *adverse circumstances* which threaten to gnaw and destroy love in the blossom.[39] [Emphasis added]

The foxes may be false prophets who spoil the vineyard. Wycliffe Bible Commentary explains, the foxes are "likely the annoyances and cares that may interfere with and damage love."[40]

This is a warning, however gently spoken, that the foxes will come. Pay attention. Listen. Take heed! Please do not dismiss this verse and move quickly to the next verse.

Wealthy landowners, in the past, made a sport of foxhunting. You might have seen pictures of "the hunt" with men on horses and a number of dogs leaving home. Foxes are serious business.

May we be as diligent as the farmers to remove the foxes from our land. This is a picture of us protecting our relationship with Christ. Let's be diligent daily.

---

[39] Carl Friedrich Keil and Franz Delitzsch, *Commentary on the Old Testament: New Updated Edition*, Electronic Database, (Peabody, MA: Hendrickson, 1996), Song of Solomon.

[40] Wycliffe Bible Commentary, (Electronic Database by Biblesoft, Inc.: Moody Press, 1962), Song of Solomon.

> Lord, help me to be constantly vigilant
> As You keep me alert to subtle things.
> May I be so alert for small hindrances
> That little foxes will never, ever cling.
>
> I want to keep my relationship with the Lord
> As consistently strong and refreshing as can be.
> Keep me so aware of those little foxes
> That nothing comes between my Beloved and Me!
>
>

The Shulamite

16 My beloved is mine, and I am his: he feedeth among the lilies.

Even though there is a temporary absence, there is an eternal, unbreakable union—a love relationship.

He feedeth among the lilies. (Song 2:16b)

She speaks highly of Him. A shepherd king probably would not feed His flocks among the lilies. So here, we have sweet poetic words describing that she knows He will return to His resting place.

We are delighted in knowing that we belong to each other.

> Knowing that I am my Beloved's is a special declaration of joy.
>
> Feeding wherever He leads me, makes belonging a privilege to enjoy!
>
> He'll feed me whenever I need it. He'll protect me as I release my will.
>
> He'll hover o'er me with fragrance. My Bridegroom, the King, loves me still.

17 Until the day break, and the shadows flee away, turn, my beloved, and be thou like a roe or a young hart upon the mountains of Bether.

"Until the day break" is a reference to the end of the day. It actually means "until the day breathe, i.e., until the fresh evening breeze spring up in what is called (Gen. 3:8) 'the cool' or breathing time of the day."[41]

"Shadows flee away" is also the evening time. The sun has set, and there are no shadows.

The mountains speak of the separation between the Shulamite and her king. She invites Him to return quickly—swiftly—leaping from peak to peak across the rocks and cliffs.

---

[41] Albert Barnes, *Barnes' Notes*, (Electronic Database by Biblesoft, Inc., 1997), Song of Solomon.

CHAPTER 2

She longs for His presence in the cool of the evening. She calls Him "my beloved."

There is none like you
No one else can touch my heart like you do.
I can search for all eternity Lord
And find, there is none like you.
(Lenny LeBlanc)

Notes

Chapter 3

The Shulamite

1 By night on my bed I sought him whom my soul loveth: I sought him, but I found him not.

This is a dream (Song 3:1-5) while she is in her bed in the night hours and in solemn contemplation. She does not say that she dreamed it; however, what she expresses could not have been a reality.

She has internal thoughts, worries, and concerns that cause the Shulamite to dream, and she is troubled. These words are her thoughts, her deep concerns, over possibly losing Him. She is fretting.

She is sincere and diligent to seek for Him, and she wanders in the city in her dream.

> Our Bridegroom is there in the nighttime. He is constantly abiding all day.
> There's no need to fret or worry. He's promised to abide and He'll stay!
> At night, when darkness surrounds me, at midnight should nightmares come,
> If confusion tries to stump me, I will constantly my Beloved obey.
>
>

2   I will rise now, and go about the city in the streets, and in the broad ways I will seek him whom my soul loveth: I sought him, but I found him not.

Here, we see that the Shulamite seeks Him in the city and in the broad ways, but she does not find Him. She is looking for her love in the wrong places. Of course, He will not be found in the streets of Jerusalem.

3   The watchmen that go about the city found me: to whom I said, Saw ye him whom my soul loveth?

She interacts with the watchmen and expresses that she is looking for Him in the city. Solomon's city is Jerusalem, and she could not have been transported there from her country home. So, this verifies that she is having a dream. She longs for Him and she feels anxious that He has left her.

Why the watchmen? The watchmen preserve the peace of the city. They check up on any disorderly conduct and assist those in need. She asks the watchmen, "Have ye seen Him whom my soul loveth?" How would the watchmen know where He is? She doesn't wait for an answer but continues on her way. The watchmen offer no guidance to her. She seeks her lover on her own.

Do you look to the watchmen to find Jesus? Will they be able to lead you to Him? Who do the watchmen represent?

4 It was but a little that I passed from them, but I found him whom my soul loveth: I held him, and would not let him go, until I had brought him into my mother's house, and into the chamber of her that conceived me.

What do you do when you cannot feel His presence? Are you able to rest in His Word and find peace? He has never forsaken you. Will you seek Him with all your heart?

5 I charge you, O ye daughters of Jerusalem, by the roes, and by the hinds of the field, that ye stir not up, nor awake my love, till he please.

The Shulamite finds Him and brings Him to her parent's house. Her dream finishes as she declares to the daughters of Jerusalem, "by the roes and hinds" meaning (by everything that is kind and gentle) to not stir or awaken her love." (This verse is repeated in Song 2:7.)

> Lord, sometimes I cannot feel Your Presence. Sometimes I feel all alone.
>
> But Your Truth will always protect me because You are my Living Stone.
>
> I'll wait and watch in Your Presence. I'll search for my Beloved until satisfied.
>
> Holding my Destiny as my Precious Lover, in Your arms I will safely abide.
>
>

A chorus of the daughters of Jerusalem

6 Who is this that cometh out of the wilderness like pillars of smoke, perfumed with myrrh and frankincense, with all powders of the merchant?

"Who is this?" is an announcement similar to "Look who is coming!" The bride coming with pillars of smoke is similar to the pillars of smoke that led the Hebrew people from Egypt and now represents the presence of the Holy Spirit in her life.

The presence and power of the Almighty God is with her as she approaches Jerusalem.

The fragrance of myrrh and frankincense speak of the suffering of Jesus and the burial of Jesus that she now carries as part of who she is. She carries this fragrance from being close to Him—from spending time with Him. She knows who she is in Christ Jesus, and she is fully anointed by the Holy Spirit; the Bride of Christ now comes to Jerusalem for the wedding.

This holy anointing not only makes her fragrant but also sets her apart. Both the power and the anointing oil have been supplied by Him.

> Lord, thank You for Your Power and Anointing.
> You have set me apart today.
> You are My Beloved and You've chosen me.
> I'm delighted to serve You every day.
>
>

7   Behold his bed, which is Solomon's; threescore valiant men are about it, of the valiant of Israel.

This bed, a royal litter, is also called a palanquin. This is a large box carried on two horizontal poles used to transport deities and royal authorities. Here is a beautiful festive procession that marches towards Jerusalem and attracts the attention of the inhabitants. The bride is being brought home with all royal honor. She has traveled through the wilderness and comes up to Jerusalem. She is surrounded by an escort for protection.

Just as the valiant men represent Solomon's guard that protects His bride, we understand that spiritually, the bride is the church of Jesus Christ and the valiant men are the angels who are appointed to watch over the souls of the bride.

Matthew Henry explains:

The church is well guarded; more are with her than against her. Lest any hurt this vineyard, God himself keeps it night and day (Isa. 27: 2, 3); particular believers, when they repose themselves in Christ and with him, though it may be night-time with them, and they may have their fears in the night, and yet safe, as Solomon set himself in the midst of his guards; the angels have a charge concerning them, ministers are appointed to watch for their souls, and they ought to be valiant men, expert in the spiritual warfare, holding the sword of the Spirit, which is the word of God, and having that gird upon their thigh, always ready to them for the silencing of the fears of God's people in the night. All the attributes of God are engaged for the safety of believers; they are kept as in a strong-hold by his power (1 Pet. 1:5); are safe in his name (Prov. 18:10), his peace protects those in whom it rules (Phil. 4:7) and the effect of righteousness in them is quietness and assurance (Isa. 32:17). Our danger is from the rulers of the darkness of this world, but we are safe in the armour of light.[42]

Believers are kept strong and safe in His name. No harm can come to His bride, day or night.

---

[42] Matthew Henry, *Matthew Henry's Commentary on the Whole Bible: New Modern Edition*, (Electronic Database by Biblesoft, Inc.: Hendrickson Publishers, Inc., 1991), Song of Solomon.

"For he shall give his angels charge over thee, to keep thee in all thy ways" (Ps. 91:11).

She is in perfect peace.

8 They all hold swords, being expert in war: every man hath his sword upon his thigh because of fear in the night.

The bride-to-be is protected as she dwells in the covering of her King. She has nothing to fear. Not even the darkness of night can cause her to fear. Darkness is a period of time when a person cannot see what is before or beside him or her. Sometimes, it is so dark that the eyes cannot adjust further. There is no light for the eyes to take in. It is pitch black.

Sons and daughters of the bride, do not fear because He and His angels (Heb. 1:14) watch over us even in the darkest of nights.

Just because the darkness comes doesn't mean that God has disappeared.

He graciously has assignments for us. Darkness comes before the dawn appears.

So let's hold steady in the darkness. Let's pray for those dear folk we know.

God has assignments for each of us. He is waiting for dawn, then He'll show.

9 King Solomon made himself a chariot of the wood of Lebanon.

This chariot is a picture of a palanquin, a bed. The finest wood of the ancient world, the wood of Lebanon, was used by King Solomon to make a chariot. This chariot or palanquin is made from a high-quality pleasantly scented wood. This wood is resistant to insects and rotting and was a popular building material for seagoing vessels and for palaces as well as an excellent source of timber for ancient woodworking.

Solomon's name signifies peace. Both the name Solomon and Shulamite have the same root letters.

This is the bride's resting place. It is a place of safety, and it is a place of strength (see Song 1:17).

I have found a resting place when sore distressed.
My Beloved has His Arms to gently caress me.
Let's remember to regularly stop and wait.
His Strength and Peace will be ours to see.

No matter which bed or resting place.
No matter if wealthy or poor.
Because I am resting in the arms of my King.
My Beloved always refreshes me for sure!

10 He made the pillars thereof of silver, the bottom thereof of gold, the covering of it of purple, the midst thereof being paved with love, for the daughters of Jerusalem.

The pillars of silver are the bedposts that hold up the bed. Silver in scripture speaks of redemption through Jesus Christ.

The bottom thereof is gold. And gold represents the deity of the Godhead. Silver, gold, and purple represent royalty.

As we rest in His love, we exude royalty. The midst thereof is covered with love.

This wood does not decay. Pillars of smoke representing the anointing of the Holy Spirit accompany this palanquin. Sixty valiant warriors defend His bride-to-be. Silver, gold, and purple are the finest of this earth; but best of all, the midst thereof is covered with love.

"Though I speak with the tongues of men and of angels, and have not charity [love], I am become as sounding brass, or a tinkling cymbal. And though I have the gift of prophecy, and understand all mysteries, and all knowledge; and though I have all faith, so that I could remove mountains, and have not charity [love], I am nothing. And though I bestow all my goods to feed the poor, and give my body to be burned, and have not charity [love], it profits me nothing" (1 Cor. 13:1–3).

Love is the pathway My Beloved offers
Let's choose to follow Him through each door.
Lord, help me to be so conscious of Your Blessings.
That I'll notice when You offer me abundantly more.

Because I'm a daughter of Your Kingdom.
Because I am the Bride of Christ.
Because we're Joint Heirs together
God has already paid my personal price.

11 Go forth, O ye daughters of Zion, and behold king Solomon with the crown wherewith his mother crowned him in the day of his espousals, and in the day of the gladness of his heart.

"Go forth," and "behold," is the challenge for the daughters of Zion, future brides-to-be, as they go out to meet the king. Their hearts are filled with joy. The king is coming, and His heart is filled with joy.

It's the day of your wedding.

Wedding Days are always special.
The Bridegroom joyfully takes His Bride.
Our wedding day will soon be coming
Then we will be thrilled to stand at His Side.

Wedding Days are fabulous. Much excitement is in the air.

Years, months and days of preparation offers tender care.

Joy is in the atmosphere. Plenty of feasting is prepared.

Love dominates every expression whenever the Lovers are there.

The Bride is prepared and ready.
The Bridegroom will make His vows.
What a picture of the great love of God,
As to Him, we'll humbly bow.

Notes

Chapter 4

The Bridegroom King

1 Behold, thou art fair, my love; behold, thou art fair; thou hast doves' eyes within thy locks: thy hair is as a flock of goats, that appear from mount Gilead.

This chapter is a conversation between Solomon and His beloved bride-to-be. She is very beautiful to him. "Thou has dove eyes" is a compliment speaking of her modesty and gentleness. Her eyes are not that of an eagle nor a hawk. Her eyes are a picture of her heart. She is sincere and honest.

The eyes are truly a window to the soul—to the heart and mind of a person. What do you see when you look in another person's eyes? Do you see gentleness and honesty? Do you see modesty or arrogance?

Her eyes are surrounded by beautiful locks of hair. Her hair is compared to a flock of goats on the mountains. This is a poetic expression. The goats are dark on the mountain, so too is her hair—dark and wavy.

2 Thy teeth are like a flock of sheep that are even shorn, which came up from the washing; whereof every one bear twins, and none is barren among them.

In the language of his time, Solomon praises her beauty by describing that his bride-to-be has beautiful teeth. The teeth are even, and none of them are missing. This is a respectful flattery of her beauty where she can be proud of herself.

Very bright white teeth reflect the light and represent her beauty. Like her eyes that are soft and like a dove, her smile is not marred by ugliness, scorn, or mockery. Her smile is sweet like her eyes.

3   Thy lips are like a thread of scarlet, and thy speech is comely: thy temples are like a piece of a pomegranate within thy locks.

The exquisite beauty of red brightens her face. Both her lips and her temples are red. A pomegranate fully ripened is red. Not only is the beauty of what Solomon sees comely, but also what Solomon hears is representative of her beauty within—her speech is comely.

Beauty with negative, condemning, criticizing words is not attractive. In Shakespeare's play, "The Taming of the Shrew," one of the characters becomes a shrew to compensate for the hurt she feels. When another character tries to tame her, she sees how childish her actions have been. Furthermore, in some television shows today, some "housewives of such-and-such state" have extremely good looks with extremely ugly speech. The words spoken from their lips are harsh, bitter, and hurtful. The words they speak do not match what one sees on the outside. Beauty and good looks do not guarantee equally good speech, but it does in His bride. The Body of Christ is not just women—It is both men and women. Our words must be fitting for the Court of the King. Harsh, cynical, and biting words; slander; bullying; and condemnation are not appropriate in the Body of Christ.

The speech of the bride of Christ must be kind and filled with grace. This represents a clean and pure heart. If one's words are impure, then "look down in their well," and you might find the stinky remains of a dead animal or some stinky experience that continues to float to the surface of their well, never forgiven and always floating on the top of their well—always spoken.

Words that are bitter and hurtful flow out of a dirty well.

The bride-to-be has a clean well. It is evident because her words are comely. She praises her King. She speaks to others of His saving grace. Her great beauty and gracious speech are truly a joy to behold.

Her temples and cheeks give her an aura of innocence. There is no guile or corruption in her.

4   Thy neck is like the tower of David builded for an armoury, whereon there hang a thousand bucklers, all shields of mighty men.

The neck spoken of here represents her inner strength. Her inner strength comes from her obedience to her Lord. There was a time when she labored in the fields and suffered, but this has not destroyed her inner strength. In fact, she is now strong.

A strong neck also speaks of single-mindedness, not a divided heart. A strong neck provides a vision that is focused.

Babies have a wobbly neck. Over time, their muscles develop to support the head and focus the vision.

The bride-to-be has a neck like a tower—It is straight and strong enough to hold a thousand shields. A straight neck does not hold a drooping head, but a head that is upright.

Like the shields hanging in an armory, the necklaces of the bride-to-be adorn her neck.

5 Thy two breasts are like two young roes that are twins, which feed among the lilies.

He praises her eyes, hair, teeth, mouth, temples, neck, and breasts—seven different parts of her body.[43] Her breasts are a pair, like young gazelles or fawns that feed among the lilies.

He has described her beauty like a passport photo or a bust, only a portrait of her from her hair to her breasts. There is no description of hands, legs, or feet. But there is sufficient description to speak of her great beauty, youth, and gentleness.

His comparison of her breasts to roes or gazelles, a class of antelopes, speaks of her innocence and beauty.

Look at the beauty of the bride of Christ— she is perfect and innocent. The bride of Christ washed in the blood of the

---

[43] Carl Friedrich Keil and Franz Delitzsch, *Commentary on the Old Testament: New Updated Edition*, Electronic Database, (Peabody, MA: Hendrickson, 1996), Song of Solomon.

Lamb is a glorious sight, without sin—chaste, pure, high in integrity, moral, and decent. This is all because of the righteousness of Christ. It is not our own righteousness, but His.

What does the Bridegroom see in her eyes when He looks upon His Love?

Goodness, gentleness, and patience are there. God has created her from above.

The Bridegroom appreciates her beauty. He is thankful for her physical parts.

But most important and best of all is that her Beloved has captured her heart.

The Shulamite

6 Until the day break, and the shadows flee away, I will get me to the mountain of myrrh, and to the hill of frankincense.

In the cool of the evening, when the day breaks, she longs for the aromatic places.

There are three events connected together in the scripture through frankincense and myrrh:

1. Frankincense and myrrh were burned to God in the temple. This fragrance ascended to God both morning and evening.

2. Frankincense and myrrh were presented to Jesus Christ on His birth (Matt. 2:11). Myrrh was used at His death (John 19:39).

3. The Shulamite longs to be with her beloved in the mountain of fragrant myrrh and the hill of frankincense.

Myrrh is bitter like someone who is mourning. Frankincense is sweet and is comparable to rejoicing.

So well depicted in this Song, long before the time of Jesus Christ, Solomon writes that the Shulamite desires to get to the mountain of myrrh and the hill of frankincense.

This mountain is spoken of in Song 2:17 and Song 8:14.

The Bridegroom King

7 Thou art all fair, my love; there is no spot in thee.

In verses 7 and 8, the bridegroom expresses His love for His spouse, His bride, and asks her to leave her mountain home; and from this point forward, live with him forever.

He expresses His love for her in the sweetest terms. It is not only her outer beauty that is appealing to him but also her inner beauty—that of her very soul.

The bride represents the church, the Body of Christ. This beauty and holiness is spoken of in Ephesians 5:26 and 27. Whereas the church, the bride is made holy by the washing with water through the Word, in that she is a radiant church, without spot or wrinkle or any blemish, but holy and blameless.

In Song 4:1, He tells her that she is fair and that she is His love, which describes her outward appearance; yet here in verse 7, He says, "There is no spot in thee." Here, He is talking about her inner soul. There are no blemishes in her. She is spotless because of Jesus Christ.

It is now (as we will see in the next verse) that He will invite her from her mountain home to live with him forevermore.

8 Come with me from Lebanon, my spouse, with me from Lebanon: look from the top of Amana, from the top of Shenir and Hermon, from the lions' dens, from the mountains of the leopards.

The king invites the bride to come and look down from the height (the top) of the mountains. Together they go up and will enjoy a spectacular view.

The names of the mountains are significant. Amana signifies firmness and fidelity and the faithful covenant established between God and His people.

Shenir is also *Senir* and is also known as Mount Hermon, which is a mountain range north of Damascus. Here, He calls her away from the world. This is the highest peak, 9,232 feet above the level of the Mediterranean Sea.

She will be delivered from her persecutors—the lions and the leopards.

He takes His bride to the mountain top. He draws her away from the cares of the world to spend time with Him.

Jesus climbed this Mount Hermon with some of His disciples and was transfigured before them.

Affirmation is important to everyone.
The Bridegroom affirms His steadfast love.
Chosen, welcomed and planned for
Soaring higher together, hand in glove!

He has invited His Beloved to rise above everything.
His Bride willingly escapes to the mountain with Him.
Transformations will take place with mountain views.
The Bridegroom is preparing new ministry for them.

---

9 Thou hast ravished my heart, my sister, my spouse; thou hast ravished my heart with one of thine eyes, with one chain of thy neck.

Ravish means to seize (archaic) and carry off, fill (literary) someone with intense delight, and enrapture.[44] It also means to enthrall, allure, enrapture, captivate, and delight.

Thou hast "hearted me"[45] or "taken away my heart" or even "subdued my heart"—His feeling is immense and overpowering as if someone has taken His heart.

Song 4:9b, "My sister, my spouse," is the first time He refers to His bride as "spouse." And to refer to His "spouse" as "sister-spouse" speaks of the purity of a sister's love combined with that of a spouse's love.[46]

One look of her eyes, perhaps a sideward glance, is enough to secure His love, His heart. One chain of her neck—like the shields hanging on David's tower—her necklace, is a beautiful ornamentation.

---

[44] *Oxford English Dictionary* Additions Series. 1997. OED Online. Oxford University Press. April 2017.

[45] Matthew Henry, *Matthew Henry's Commentary on the Whole Bible: New Modern Edition*, (Electronic Database by Biblesoft, Inc.: Hendrickson Publishers, Inc., 1991), Song of Solomon.

[46] Robert Jamieson, A.R. Fausset & David Brown, *Jamieson, Fausset, and Brown Commentary* (Electronic Database by Biblesoft, Inc., 1997), Song of Solomon.

Proverbs 1:2–9 says that there are four spiritual chains that one receives from God:

1. The fear of the Lord.
2. Hearing instruction of father and mother.
3. Wise to listen and receive discipline.
4. Understanding and doing the Word of God.

Lord, thank You for the spiritual chains
That daily bind me to your loving self.
Thank You Lord, for paying the price.
You could have left me on a shelf.

You taught me well, how to fear You.
You brought those who cared, who could teach.
You taught me to listen and obey Your Voice
Now I will try to apply wisdom to folk I can reach.

10 How fair is thy love, my sister, my spouse! How much better is thy love than wine! And the smell of thine ointments than all spices!

CHAPTER 4

He continues to praise her beauty—the fragrance of her clothing, her warm dove eyes, and her lips that speak words like honey. He inhales her beauty.[47]

Clothed in garments of righteousness carrying the sweet fragrance of the Spirit of the Lord, she is pleasing to the Lord. Her garments and fragrance are visible to all for they speak of her relationship with Christ.

11 Thy lips, O my spouse, drop as the honeycomb: honey and milk are under thy tongue; and the smell of thy garments is like the smell of Lebanon.

An impressive sight—her eyes, necklace, fragrance, and clothing and her lips that speak sweet words. The lips He kisses are like milk and honey, speaking of her purity. Her voice is sweet, seasoned with grace.

The fresh fragrance of her garments is like the smell of the outdoors—the fragrance of Lebanon.

---

[47] Carl Friedrich Keil and Franz Delitzsch, *Commentary on the Old Testament: New Updated Edition*, Electronic Database, (Peabody, MA: Hendrickson, 1996), Song of Solomon.

The Bridegroom regularly acknowledges His
Bride's beauty.
Her fragrance is obvious everywhere.
Lord keep us so close to the Bridegroom that
Our personality is influenced by prayer.

May our relationships become so focused
That everyone we meet is drawn to You.
Help us to represent You so well that
Godliness becomes our predominant view.

12 A garden enclosed is my sister, my spouse; a spring shut up, a fountain sealed.

She is closed away as a pleasant garden and no one has access to her. This garden has an eternal fountain in it, a fountain of life-giving water to nourish the splendid plants. She belongs exclusively to Him!

She is separated from the common. The hedge of protection around her keeps her safe from predators.

Jesus Christ is her living water. "But whosoever drinketh of the water that I shall give him shall never thirst; but the water that I shall give him shall be in him a well of water springing up into everlasting life" (John 4:14).

"He that believeth on me, as the scripture hath said, out of his belly shall flow rivers of living water" (John 7:38).

Soon, she will give living water to others.

13 Thy plants are an orchard of pomegranates, with pleasant fruits; camphire, with spikenard.

All kinds of exotic plants and fruits surround her, and she is enclosed in a garden—protected.

There is nothing in this garden that is unpleasant. Fruits, spices, and fragrant scents abound. The flowers, fruits, and spices are a "flower-language of love" surrounding His bride-to-be.

As one considers the fruits and flowers of the next verse, ask yourself this question: Are we like the lily or the saffron, carrying the fragrance of Christ with the Holy Spirit abiding in us?

14 Spikenard and saffron; calamus and cinnamon, with all trees of frankincense; myrrh and aloes, with all the chief spices:

These are seven of the most precious spices. Here are some of scripture verses where these spices are spoken of.

In the New Testament spikenard is costly. "And being in Bethany in the house of Simon the leper; as He sat at meat, there came a woman having an alabaster box of ointment of spikenard very precious; and she brake the box, and poured it on his head" (Mark 14:3).

Saffron are the flowers possessing a sweet honey-like fragrance. The color and fragrance are concentrated in the red stigmata. The threadlike stigmata are a vivid crimson color that emerge from the center of each flower.

In the Old Testament, calamus is one of the ingredients of the holy anointing oil.

> "Take thou also unto thee principal spices, of pure myrrh five hundred shekels, and of sweet cinnamon half so much, even two hundred and fifty shekels, and of sweet calamus two hundred and fifty shekels, And of cassia five hundred shekels after the shekel of the sanctuary, and of oil olive an hin. And thou shalt make an oil of holy ointment, an ointment compound after the art of the apothecary: it shall be an holy anointing oil." (Exod. 30: 23-25)

Cinnamon has a naturally sweet taste without sugar. Not only is it a beautiful fragrant tree, but it has health-giving properties.

Frankincense is the resin from a tree that gives off a "frank" odor when it burns and is one of the ingredients in the perfume of the sanctuary. It was used to accompany an offering to the Lord (Lev. 24:7).

Myrrh is one of the ingredients of holy oil. It has been used for the beautification of women (Esther 2:12). In several passages, it is used as a perfume, and it is a gift to baby Jesus. When a tree is cut, it gives forth a sap or a resin. The sap hardens into beads. Similar to frankincense, myrrh is also a resin. It gives off a fragrant odor.

Aloes is an agarwood used in incense and perfume. It is formed in the heart of *Aquilaria agallochum*. The costly gum or resin is extracted from the wood of the tree.

Some of the plants are not only beautiful and fragrant but have healing properties as well.

His bride-to-be, who is altogether lovely, stands in the middle of fresh exotic spices, fresh fruits and flowers. She breathes in fresh mountain air and sparkling water springs forth in the garden for her to drink.

The writer, anointed by the Holy Spirit, included the finest things of the earth and put them together in one garden, in a pure place, apart from the world.

By faith, we rise up and come away to His garden to be refreshed. We have His Spirit. We take on His fragrance.

15 A fountain of gardens, a well of living waters, and streams from Lebanon.

Fresh, crystal-clear waters from the snowy tops of Mount Lebanon supply the springs. Yet, to the king, His bride-to-be has become like a fresh-flowing stream and fountain with pure water. The water gives life to the splendid garden. Living waters are life-giving and abundant.

It is interesting to note that John 7:38 says, "He that believeth on me, as the scripture hath said, out of his belly shall flow rivers of living water." She has learned to be like him and provide living water.

According to Psalm 36:8 and 9, "They shall be abundantly satisfied with the fatness of thy house; and thou shalt make them drink of the river of thy pleasures. For with thee is the fountain of life: in thy light shall we see light."

> Lord, may I be such a reservoir of Your Goodness that folk become revived once again.
> May the rivers and waters flow freely until Your anointing cascades like fresh rain.
>
>

The Shulamite

16 Awake, O north wind; and come, thou south; blow upon my garden, that the spices thereof may flow out. Let my beloved come into his garden, and eat his pleasant fruits.

She speaks. Awake. She speaks first to the wind, which in scripture is representative of the Holy Spirit of God. Through the scripture, we see that the spices represent prayer and praise, adoration, and affection to the Lord.

The wind is the Holy Spirit. The North and the South wind swirl together, like a mighty wind as on the day of Pentecost.

The North wind is typically the cold wind, just as the South wind is typically the hot wind. When two fronts converge, it causes a swirling effect. The winds meet and swirl. In the swirling winds, the fragrant aroma arises. The fragrance of her prayers and praise arise to her beloved. It is obvious that the Holy Spirit helps her manifest her love for the king.

And she says, "Let my beloved come into his garden and eat his pleasant fruits."

Refreshing winds are blowing in God's garden. Prayer and Praise offer sweet spices there.

Adoration and love for my Beloved Redeemer mingle in God's gardens everywhere.

Let us rise and be about our Beloved's business. Let's linger in His Presence to be blessed.

Let's joyfully welcome the Holy Spirit as we fellowship with other souls that need rest.

Notes

Chapter 5

Bridegroom King

1 I am come into my garden, my sister, my spouse: I have gathered my myrrh with my spice; I have eaten my honeycomb with my honey; I have drunk my wine with my milk: eat, O friends; drink, yea, drink abundantly, O beloved.

Here is the union of love; the consummation of marriage. The Lord has come into His garden. She requested him to come in verse 4:16, and He has come. What a beautiful picture of love. She has longed for him, and He is now here. He has now obtained possession of His garden.

Eating and drinking are representative of the enjoyment of love. This verse is the climax of the *Song of Solomon.*

Longing to be loved is a natural, human need. It's a desire God has placed within.

Our Beloved shelters, protects and cares for us. We're protected from the enemy and sin.

We've waited with anticipation and wonder. We've longed for this day to come.

Now our Beloved has claimed us. We are graciously bound together as one.

The Shulamite Bride

2 I sleep, but my heart waketh: it is the voice of my beloved that knocketh, saying, Open to me, my sister, my love, my dove, my undefiled: for my head is filled with dew, and my locks with the drops of the night.

This is like the beginning, Song 2:2–7, in the bride's dream where she is longing for her bridegroom. "I sleep, but my heart waketh" (Song 5: 2a) is the same as saying "I dream."

He might have traveled a long way to return to her because His locks are filled with dew.

The bride has fallen asleep. We do not know how much time has passed since the wedding, but she has a dream, just as she does in Song 3:1–4. Have her affections cooled or was she resting and letting him keep watch?

Suddenly, she hears the voice of her beloved calling her with the kindest, sweetest words as He knocks at her door: "Open to me, my sister, my love, my dove, my undefiled." Yet she doesn't rise. She remains in her warm bed.

Her Lord calls tenderly for her to "open."

When the Lord calls to you, are you willing to open the door?

Lord, help me to be willing to open all doors to You.

Whenever You Call, I'll be ready. What a joy to be called by You.

3 I have put off my coat; how shall I put it on? I have washed my feet; how shall I defile them?

The bride makes excuses. She does not say, "I will not get up." She says, "How shall I..." It is her excuse that keeps her from the bridegroom. She doesn't want to get her feet dirty. She doesn't want to get up and get dressed. She is not willing to leave the warmth of her bed and bother herself.

What she will not do in real life is now a part of her dream, and it exposes who she truly is. And yet, as she thinks to reject him, she comes to her senses.

Lord, forgive me for making excuses.
Forgive me for my selfish thoughts.
Knowing the privileges in store for me.
I'm thankful my laziness has been caught.

4   My beloved put in his hand by the hole of the door, and my bowels were moved for him.

To think that she is in her bed and watching him put His hand in the hole of the door and she does not jump out of her bed gives one a feeling of sadness. Of course, she feels deeply for her beloved! He shows her His hand to move her from her indifference. Has the Lord ever shown you His hand to move you from indifference?

It is enough to see His hand. Oh, how He longs for her as He shows forth His hand inside the door. Will you open?

Lord, Open my eyes to my daily laziness.
Forgive for wanting to snuggle in bed.
You *never* sleep or even slumber.
You're lovingly pursuing me instead.

5   I rose up to open to my beloved; and my hands dropped with myrrh, and my fingers with sweet smelling myrrh, upon the handles of the lock.

His hands were anointed with myrrh when He touched the door, and now, her hands drop with the fragrance of Him.

He has arrived at her door and left evidence of His standing at the door calling to her in tender words, "my sister, my love, my spouse." Grace gives her the ability to move from her bed.

> My hands are covered with Your Fragrance.
> Your arrival fills me with joy.
> Your Grace is sufficient to forgive me.
> Your Presence is mine to enjoy.
>
>

6 I opened to my beloved; but my beloved had withdrawn himself, and was gone: my soul failed when he spake: I sought him, but I could not find him; I called him, but he gave me no answer.

She didn't open at first and now, as Matthew Henry relates, is "the most melancholy part of the story."[48] She misses him because she is coming to the door too late. She heard His voice and didn't move immediately.

We must be ready for Him. We must be listening for His voice. We must rise when He calls.

---

[48] Matthew Henry, *Matthew Henry's Commentary on the Whole Bible: New Modern Edition*, (Electronic Database by Biblesoft, Inc.: Hendrickson Publishers, Inc., 1991), Song of Solomon.

She has the memory of His words that He spoke to her, and she carries the fragrance of Him from the precious oil that He left on the lock of the door.

> My Beloved's Fragrance is an impression in my nostrils.
> His love has suffered my dreadful, sad neglect.
> Forgive me Lord for my annoying laziness.
> My tardiness has made me feel like a wreck.
>
> I need the fragrance of Your Presence.
> I need to breathe in Your fresh air.
> When I become saturated in Your Presence.
> My life becomes an example of Your Care.
>
>

7   The watchmen that went about the city found me, they smote me, they wounded me; the keepers of the walls took away my veil from me.

She arrived at the city on a palanquin, as a queen; and now, she is treated as a common woman. Her veil, *radad*, is a full-length overgarment similar to a coat, a shawl, or a "wrapper."[49]

---

[49]   Carl Friedrich Keil and Franz Delitzsch, *Commentary on the Old Testament: New Updated Edition*, Electronic Database, (Peabody, MA: Hendrickson, 1996), Song of Solomon.

The watchmen smote her because they think she is a woman of the street. But her love compels her to look for her bridegroom. What does your love compel you to do?

Do you keep the Lord in close communion every day, or do you busy yourself with other things, thinking of Him fondly but never spending time with Him? Will you seek Him out at any cost?

What does God's love compel you to do?
Will you commune with Him every day?
Will you find a place of holy quietness?
No matter the cost. Do it *now*. Don't delay.

Love for your Bridegroom is a priority.
Love for His Fragrance can become real.
Lord, help us to faithfully take time for You
Because intimacy with You offers appeal.

8 I charge you, O daughters of Jerusalem, if ye find my beloved, that ye tell him, that I am sick of love.

She turns from the watchmen to the women, a more humble group. The watchmen were harsh with her, but she can relate to the "daughters of Jerusalem." She hopes to gain sympathy with the women concerning her lovesickness. They had, no doubt, attended her wedding and would be sympathetic. Are we sensitive when Christ withdraws?

King David wrote:

> Create in me a clean heart, O God;
> And renew a right spirit within me.
> Cast me not away from your presence;
> And take not thy holy spirit from me.
> (Ps. 51:10, 11)

Even King David did not want to be without the presence of the Lord.

Have we done anything to provoke him to withdraw, or have we laid in bed and not moved when He knocked at our door—the door of our heart?

Let's be cheerful and seek His presence daily! If we have sinned by laziness or actions, let us repent and turn back to Him.

Only then will the joy of our salvation return. He will give us a willing spirit to sustain us. "Restore unto me the joy of thy salvation; and uphold me with thy free spirit" (Ps. 51:12).

A chorus of the daughters of Jerusalem

9   What is thy beloved more than another beloved, O thou fairest among women? what is thy beloved more than another beloved, that thou dost so charge us?

The daughters of Jerusalem refer to her as the "fairest among women." She is beautiful to her Lord and to society. She is truly beautiful made in His image and a reflection of Him—a reflection of His love for her.

The daughters of Jerusalem ask her questions about her beloved, and as we will read, she is ready to speak about her beloved.

> Am I prepared to speak for My Beloved?
> Am I ready to give an intimate report?
> Do I exemplify His loving Personality?
> Honoring my Beloved always has import.

The Shulamite Bride

10 My beloved is white and ruddy, the chiefest among ten thousand.

The word "white" is the Hebrew root word *tsch*, from the word *tsaachach*. This means dazzling, sunny, and bright. It is poorly translated as "white" when it is really describing that her beloved is brilliant like the sun.[50]

---

50 Carl Friedrich Keil and Franz Delitzsch, *Commentary on the Old Testament: New Updated Edition*, Electronic Database, (Peabody, MA: Hendrickson, 1996), Song of Solomon.

When Jesus was transfigured, "his raiment was white as the light." "And was transfigured before them: and his face did shine as the sun, and his raiment was white as the light" (Matt. 17:2).

He radiates light, a dazzling bright light yet He is man, and among ten thousand, He is easily found. She can spot him in a crowd.

11 His head is as the most fine gold, his locks are bushy, and black as a raven.

Pure gold radiates beauty. All of the impurities are gone; the gold is pure.

His black hair drops from His head. It is bushy like "the waving branches of a palm tree,"[51] free-flowing, shiny hair with curls or locks.

The King of Kings presents as a perfect man, radiant and distinguished above all others. His head of gold represents His sovereignty. His free-flowing bushy curls drop from His head.

Matthew Henry describes that "His head speaks of His dominion over all, and His influence upon His church and its members."[52]

---

[51] Albert Barnes, *Barnes' Notes*, (Electronic Database by Biblesoft, Inc., 1997), Song of Solomon.

[52] Matthew Henry, *Matthew Henry's Commentary on the Whole Bible: New Modern Edition*, (Electronic Database by Biblesoft, Inc.: Hendrickson Publishers, Inc., 1991), Song of Solomon.

12 His eyes are as the eyes of doves by the rivers of waters, washed with milk, and fitly set.

A dove's eyes are gentle and tender. Some people have eyes that are playful, while others' eyes are intense; some have angry eyes; and others have laughing eyes. The eyes of the bridegroom are gentle. Fitly set and moistened eyes means that the eyes are youthful and not dry. Fresh eyes rather than dry crusty eyes set perfectly in place.

Slow down this week and take the time to look into people's eyes. What do you see? What do you think is behind their eyes? What is their story? Do the eyes and the words match?

Spend time with your Lord. You will find that His eyes are eyes of love and His words are words of love. The King of Kings loves you, and He wants to speak words of love to you. He is lovely.

> Am I receptive to my Beloved Bridegroom's wooing?
> Am I ready to become intimately involved?
> Or do I take my Bridegroom for granted?
> His protection will all my apprehension dissolve.
>
>

13 His cheeks are as a bed of spices, as sweet flowers: his lips like lilies, dropping sweet smelling myrrh.

There are eleven descriptions of her beloved.

1. Beloved is white and ruddy—dazzling.
2. Head of gold.
3. Locks are bushy and black.
4. Eyes as dove's eyes.
5. Cheeks like spices/flowers.
6. Lips like lilies.
7. Hands are as gold rings.
8. Belly as ivory with sapphires.
9. Legs as pillars of marble.
10. Countenance—excellent as cedars.
11. Mouth—sweet.

She describes His beauty in such a lovely way and in such a respectful way. One's lips are never described as lilies unless the words behind them are pure, beautiful, and life-giving. His words are life-giving and sweet. His cheeks radiate life and tenderness.

Are you overwhelmed by His good qualities? Have you come to see His excellence? He is your bridegroom. He is incorruptible.

14 His hands are as gold rings set with the beryl: his belly is as bright ivory overlaid with sapphires.

He has beautiful, elegant fingers. The beryl is a most alluring and popular mineral. It occurs in many colors, with many gemstone varieties. Here, it is probably a gold tone. It does not say He wears gold rings, but His hands "are as" gold rings.

The nails of His fingers are set like jewels in a ring. His belly is bright like ivory—sturdy, strong, and shiny. The sapphires are on His belt or waistband. He is steadfast and full of compassion.[53] His clothing is ornamented with sapphires. Sapphires are pink, purple, green, orange and blue in color.

> God created color for our enjoyment.
> God blessed us all with different hues.
> Lord, help me to appreciate Your Majesty.
> When beautiful shades come into my view.
>
>

15 His legs are as pillars of marble, set upon sockets of fine gold: his countenance is as Lebanon, excellent as the cedars.

---

[53] Robert Jamieson, A.R. Fausset & David Brown, *Jamieson, Fausset, and Brown Commentary* (Electronic Database by Biblesoft, Inc., 1997), Song of Solomon.

His legs are pillars of marble, speaking that they are strong and steadfast, set upon sockets of fine gold—speaking of His majesty and magnificence. His legs are steady and supportive. His countenance shows His demeanor. His appearance shows forth His loveliness.

His head is compared to a mountain near Jerusalem. This mountain is tall and majestic.

"The righteous flourish like the palm tree and grow like the cedars in Lebanon" (Ps. 92:12). He is incorruptible.

16 His mouth is most sweet: yea, he is altogether lovely. This is my beloved, and this is my friend, O daughters of Jerusalem.

His mouth is sweet; he is lovely; this is my beloved; this is my friend. Oh, how she introduces her beloved! Of all the attributes, the sweetest is His mouth. His breath produces words that are tender and kind, uplifting and sweet. She is drawn by His kisses, but she is first drawn by His tender words. The way that He speaks to her is altogether lovely. His speech portrays His personality. She declares, "This is my beloved." "This is my friend." She knows Him, and she is assured that He is her friend, her beloved. She has decided that He is her choice.

"O taste and see that the *Lord* is good: blessed is the man the trusteth in him" (Ps. 24:8).

Lord, Your Mouth is uniquely special.
You spoke this world into being one day.
Your mouth also offered us forgiveness
On dark Calvary in a unique and loving way.

The Bridegroom speaks to His Beloved.
With whispered tones of loving praise.
His words captivate her personality.
His love is expressed in unique ways.

Her Beloved's Kisses draw her closer to Him.
She never tires of His all-Embracing Love.
Her innocence is captured in every caress
His motivation is designed by God above.

Notes

Chapter 6

A chorus of the daughters of Jerusalem

1 Whither is thy beloved gone, O thou fairest among women? whither is thy beloved turned aside? that we may seek him with thee.

My KJV Thompson Chain-Reference Bible begins Chapter Six with this heading "The church professes her faith in Christ."[54]

If you had described your beloved to another, would it have been a description that not only spoke of your love and His beauty but also spoke of your hope in Him? Do you have faith in Him?

Children, spouses, friends, and coworkers are watching your life. Are you in love with Jesus, or are you pretending? Have you compartmentalized your communication to your bridegroom into two-30 second prayers a week, and those prayers are only to ask for blessing and protection? Has your relationship with Him grown in the last year or has it diminished?

---

54   Thompson's ChainReference Bible, (Thompson's Chain Reference Bible Staff, B. B. Kirkbride Bible Company, Inc., 1998), Song of Solomon.

The Shulamite Bride

2 My beloved is gone down into his garden, to the beds of spices, to feed in the gardens, and to gather lilies.

After your long search, you have news of where your Beloved is to be found. He gives of Himself and sometimes He withdraws himself, and you will learn to trust him and his desires.[55] He knows best. You will want what pleases Him.

He takes delight in His garden and flowers. There is a higher interest here than that of the beauty of flowers. Here is a state of loveliness and thoughtfulness. It is in "this state of loveliness" that Verse 3 begins.

3 I am my beloved's and my beloved is mine: he feedeth among the lilies.

You are totally His. There is no more self-seeking. There is no more self-loathing. You are freed from that. "You have given yourself without reserve and you belong to Him."[56]

Suddenly, you realize that you sparkle with joy. There is no going back. You will always love Him. There is nothing else that is more satisfying. He is your all-in-all. You experience such joy and delight in Him. His gentleness and sweet fragrance are as

55 Jeanne Guyon, *Song of Songs: Explanations and Reflections Regarding the Deeper Christian Life.* (Jacksonville, FL: The Seed Sowers, 1980), 87.
56 Ibid, 88.

a garden of lilies. Nothing can be compared to the sweetness of Him.

His love melts the icicles of your past experiences. You are warmed in His presence. You are one with Him.

> Because I am My Beloved's, I can enter God's Garden with Him.
>
> Access to the beauty around us is another blessing that never dims.
>
> Icicles of life's passed experiences will be replaced with warmth from above.
>
> Now because I'm accepted in the Beloved, I can sparkle with His Joy and Love.
>
>

The Bridegroom King

4 Thou art beautiful, O my love, as Tirzah, comely as Jerusalem, terrible as an army with banners.

The two beautiful cities in the land were Tirzah and Jerusalem. These cities were pleasing to the king.

Jerusalem, for the Israelites, was beautiful, but why Tirzah? Tirzah means *pleasant.*[57] Tirzah was a beautiful region high on a

---

57 Robert Jamieson, A.R. Fausset & David Brown, *Jamieson, Fausset, and Brown Commentary* (Electronic Database by Biblesoft, Inc., 1997), Song of Solomon.

hill, in a region of olive trees, and so was Jerusalem. Both cities were high in elevation.

To be both beautiful and terrible seems to be a contradiction. Her personality is strong and irresistible. Armies with their banners show forth victory and confidence. And so, the appearance of Shulamite is strikingly beautiful and awesome, like an army with banners. Invincible!

As you completely abandon yourself to God, He gives you His beauty. He will preserve your purity! You are a co-owner of His inheritance.[58] He dwells in you, and you dwell in Him. You are beautiful, and the enemy fears you because you are anointed of God. You are His beloved.

Since God gives us His beauty and He preserves our purity, are we to take charge of our bodies? Or are we to abandon ourselves to God, and He will take care of "fixing" us up and making us presentable?

I think both. We are to abandon ourselves to God. We are dependent on Him for every aspect of our lives. Yet we are to strive to preserve our purity. There is so much in the world that can dirty our lives. A white glove can fall into the mud, but it is never said that the "mud became glovey." We must strive to not become muddy and to preserve our minds from what we see, and hear on a daily basis.

---

[58] Jeanne Guyon, *Song of Songs: Explanations and Reflections Regarding the Deeper Christian Life*. (Jacksonville, FL: The Seed Sowers, 1980), 89.

5 Turn away thine eyes from me, for they have overcome me: thy hair is as a flock of goats that appear from Gilead.

The great beauty of the bride is like an army with banners, terrible and awesome; and here, she is also irresistible. "The bride's eyes pierced the heart of the bridegroom."[59]

To have the eyes "overcome" Him is the word *rahab* from the Hebrew root word ראהאב.

Rahab means to be impetuous, or that the eyes "strongly press" upon me.[60]

He continues to describe His bride as He did earlier in Chapters 2 and 4. Here begins a repetition Verses 5b and through verse 7.

6 Thy teeth are as a flock of sheep which go up from the washing, whereof every one beareth twins, and there is not one barren among them.

His love is unchanged; His words of praise are the same; He desires no one other than her.

Recognize the reality of His love for you. He repeats words of praise and reassures of His love. Repetition speaks of a love that is greater than on day one when He first told her. Just as He continues in His affection for her, our Lord continues in His affection towards you. Should He need to repeat His words, He

---

59   Adam Clarke, *Adam Clarke's Commentary*, (Electronic Database by Biblesoft Electronic Inc., 1996), Song of Solomon.

most certainly will. What kind of love is this? This is enduring love! Repetitious love!

> Repetition in scripture frequently creates an emphasis to think about.
> The Bride with her beauty and innocence reminds us without a doubt.
>
> Do you ever wonder how God could love you?
> Do you ever question why God even cares?
> Remember, dear precious Pilgrim,
> God loves you and hears every prayer.
>
>

7   As a piece of a pomegranate are thy temples within thy locks.

Beautiful in holiness is the bride of Christ; here, her cheeks are compared to the pomegranate, red and lovely. The outward appearance of the pomegranate is red, and the inside is like ruby jewels. Could this have a deeper meaning here?

If so, her heart and inward parts are even more beautiful than her outward appearance—just like the pomegranate.

She is respected in the eyes of the world for her outward beauty, but her inward beauty far excels the ordinary ones of the world. She has hidden strength.

> Do you ever wonder, dear Pilgrim, how you find the strength to go on?
> In the wisdom of the Holy Spirit, He creates power because you belong.
>
> He also gave you inner beauty. He gave you His Strength and His Song.
> He's not going to change His Agenda, even when Satan tries to do you wrong.
>
> So pick up God's beauty from your ashes. Remember whose Child you are!
> God has already planned your future. With your Bridegroom you'll travel far!

8 There are threescore queens, and fourscore concubines, and virgins without number.

9 My dove, my undefiled is but one; she is the only one of her mother, she is the choice one of her that bare her. The daughters saw her, and blessed her; yea, the queens and the concubines, and they praised her.

Here, she is compared with the others. They may be affiliated with her, but they are not the bride. Which group are you in? Do you long for Him but have made only a little progress towards Him, or have you given yourself over completely and find your greatest joy in the bridegroom?

Are you one of His favorites, or do you barely know Him? Does He know you? Close your door to the world. Spend some one-to-one time with Jesus in your prayer closet.

> Spending time alone with Jesus is the best way to learn His Will.
> How much time are you investing, or is your time with Him almost nil?
> Close the door to life's distractions. Prioritize time with Him every day.
> Jesus and you alone together is the best way to learn His ways.
>
>

10 Who is she that looketh forth as the morning, fair as the moon, clear as the sun, and terrible as an army with banners?

She is as beautiful as the morning light, and in the night, she is as the moon-reflecting light. She reflects His light.

Her banners are victory banners. She is formidable.

Who is she?   She is the beloved.

The darling of her mother.

She is as lovely as the dawn.

She shines pure and bright.

The Church, the Body of Christ, are the "excellent ones of the earth."[60]

Lord, help us to always reflect Your Goodness. May we always shine for You.

Keep us wise and approachable as we link arms all our lives through.

The Shulamite Bride

11 I went down into the garden of nuts to see the fruits of the valley, and to see whether the vine flourished, and the pomegranates budded.

The garden is a quiet place for meditation for her in the country, remembering that He met with her in the garden. Oh, how she loves His presence in the garden. She goes down into the garden to check the fruit of the vine. She desires the garden to be fruitful.

Ask God to help you lay aside those sins that keep you from being fruitful and victorious. Meet with Him in the garden and let Him pour out His Holy Spirit upon you. Ask for forgiveness

---

[60] Matthew Henry, *Matthew Henry's Commentary on the Whole Bible: New Modern Edition*, (Electronic Database by Biblesoft, Inc.: Hendrickson Publishers, Inc., 1991), Song of Solomon.

for any sin that keeps you from His presence– even the sin of busyness.

> Lord, sometimes I need to go back again. Perhaps back the way I came.
> I've become so busy with busyness that I am neglecting to call on Your Name.
>
> Take me back to the beginning. Remind me of what You have done.
> Thank You, Lord, for saving me and for the precious gift of Your Son.
>
> Once again, pour Your Spirit upon me. Once again refresh my tired, busy soul.
> Alone with You and my memories. Your refreshing Presence has made me whole.
>
>

12 Or ever I was aware, my soul made me like the chariots of Amminadib.

Amminadib is more than likely a noble person who drove a swift chariot.

Very quickly, swiftly, she desires to return to Him. Why hesitate? Why delay? Your love for Him; your desires, thoughts, and prayers; and your time invested daily will carry you back to Him.

May your prayers be as chariots of fire.

> "And ye shall seek me, and find *me*, when ye shall search for me with all your heart. And I will be found of you, saith the LORD: and I will turn away your captivity, and I will gather you from all the nations, and from all the places whither I have driven you, saith the LORD; and I will bring you again into the place whence I caused you to be carried away captive" (Jer. 29:13, 14).

Lord, offer me a chariot of fire, as I speedily rush into Your Arms.

Forgive me for the distractions of living. May my prayer prevent sinful harm?

I'm returning to the arms of my Bridegroom. I'm remembering the joy I once had.

Thank You, Lord, for your welcoming caress. My refreshed soul is no longer sad.

A chorus of the daughters of Jerusalem

13 Return, return, O Shulamite; return, return, that we may look upon thee. What will ye see in the Shulamite? As it were the company of two armies.

Four times she is called to "return," to come back. The daughters want to see her grace, beauty, and strength one more time and they want to see her dance.

The Shulamite Bride

> What will ye see in the Shulamite?
> (Song 6:13b).

The bride asks, "What will you see in me?"

The Bridegroom King

> As it were the company of two armies
> (Song 6:13c).

These "two armies" are two hosts in a place named Mahanaim. Mahanaim means a place of two camps.[61] These two hosts are referred to in Genesis 32:2, as the angelic hosts and Jacob and

---

[61] Robert Jamieson, A.R. Fausset & David Brown, *Jamieson, Fausset, and Brown Commentary* (Electronic Database by Biblesoft, Inc., 1997), Song of Solomon.

his camp. And when Jacob saw them, he said, This is God's host: and he called the name of that place Mahanaim.

A city was built there afterward. Mahanaim is where Jacob had a visitation of angels and is known as the place where He experienced great victory in prayer. The dance of Mahanaim is a well-known sacred dance, taking its name from the locality in which the dance originated (Gen. 32:2; Josh. 21:38).[62]

Because of the history of Mahanaim and the visitation of angels, this dance is called the "dance of angels." (This city was also known to be a sanctuary city. King David fled to this place when his son Absalom rebelled.) Shulamite begins to dance the dance of Mahanaim.

> Lord, thank you that we can return to You with feet that dance with joy.
> Sanctuaries are places with You, where healing and peace we enjoy.
>
> Lord, keep us dancing with joy today. Help us to make melody in our hearts.
> The joy of the Lord gives the strength we need. Your love will never depart.
>
>

---

[62] Albert Barnes, *Barnes' Notes*, (Electronic Database by Biblesoft, Inc., 1997), Song of Solomon.

Notes

Chapter 7

The Bridegroom King

1 How beautiful are thy feet with shoes, O prince's daughter! The joints of thy thighs are like jewels, the work of the hands of a cunning workman.

Remember in Song 4:1–5 that He describes his bride, but only from her chest to the top of her head? Here, the bridegroom describes her from her feet upward. Her feet are praised. The bride is dancing, and her movement is graceful. She is called the "prince's daughter." She has been raised in rank because the king has betrothed Himself to her. Her status is the image-bearer of the King of Kings. She is no longer a child. She is now an heir.

Her joints are like jewels made by a cunning workman. Her thighs and the circular movement of her thighs are compared to jewels on an ornamental chain that swings freely.

Let's walk in dignity and bring honor to God. Let's not bring shame to Jesus.

Dancing is one way to praise Him.
Singing offers melodies too.
However, the Lord seeks to ignite you.
Let's praise Him in all that we do.

2 Thy navel is like a round goblet, which wanteth not liquor: thy belly is like a heap of wheat set about with lilies.

The navel speaks of the innermost part where life springs from, and as Matthew Henry says, "the belly speaks to the spiritual prosperity of a believer."[63] The center of her body is described delicately and beautifully. It is round like a wine glass (goblet); her belly is like a heap of wheat, already "sifted"[64], and in a heap surrounded by lilies.

Her dress must be magnificent with the roundness of her waist showing through her garment as she dances.

Life will spring from her. The Creator has placed everything in her that she needs—His beautiful creation. From her, life will spring forth with the Father's spark of life. So too the church gives birth with the Father's life-giving person, the Holy Spirit.

---

[63] Matthew Henry, *Matthew Henry's Commentary on the Whole Bible: New Modern Edition*, (Electronic Database by Biblesoft, Inc.: Hendrickson Publishers, Inc., 1991), Song of Solomon.

[64] Carl Friedrich Keil and Franz Delitzsch, *Commentary on the Old Testament: New Updated Edition*, Electronic Database, (Peabody, MA: Hendrickson, 1996), Song of Solomon.

Be confident. God has placed everything you need within, and you are magnificent in His eyes.

> Everything we need is from the Father. His attachment offers life renewed.
> From the very center of our being, His strength always flows towards you.
>
> Depend upon the Savior to bless you. Depend upon nourishment from His Word.
> Depend on His Children to encourage. What encouragement from you, have folk heard?
>
> Remind folk to be confident in the Bridegroom. Speak about the new birth for lost souls.
> Spring forth with joy and contentment. Share the blessing of God's heavenly goals.
>
>

3 Thy two breasts are like two young roes that are twins.

See the notes in Song 4:5.

Your breasts are life-giving, and you have the ability to nourish others. Your ability is likened to two young roes. Be watchful and attend to others in need.

Go first to Christ and strengthen yourself, and let His grace flow through you to others.

> Lord, may my life offer nourishment to those who my pathway crosses.
> Help me to be alert to your leading, no matter the need or the costs.
>
> Lord, I come to you, knowing you'll strengthen me as a loving mother feeds her child,
> Lord, help me to always be lovingly nourished by thee, even if my assignment is wild.
>
> You know what's ahead. You know other folks needs.
> May I always and lovingly seek to plant seeds.

4 Thy neck is as a tower of ivory; thine eyes like the fishpools in Heshbon, by the gate of Bath-rabbim: thy nose is as the tower of Lebanon which looketh toward Damascus.

At the beginning of the Song of Songs, we pictured the bride dark from working in the field. Now, she is bright and strong like ivory. What a contrast! Her neck is as an ivory tower. She is strong. Her faith is strong. She is now able to withstand attack. She is unconquerable.

Compared to the freshwater that flows into the fish pools and glistens in the sun, so too are her eyes, sparkling and moist. These fish pools must have been magnificent near the gate of the city. A study of gates of the cities would tell us they would provide a point of controlled access, to pay taxes, to charge tolls, to provide legal information, and to defend and secure the city.

The Brandenburg Gate in Berlin, a landmark in Germany, was built on the site of a former city gate. It marked the start of the road from Berlin to Brandenburg.

The gate of Bath-rabbim must have been a real tourist spot with fish pools near the gate or place of gathering. No doubt, water flowed in freely to keep the pools clean.

Her nose is described as a tower of Lebanon. Jamieson explains that "her nose implies discernment."[65] Certainly, her nose represents sound judgment for she is unable to be turned aside.

Her eyes are discerning, and she has spiritual insight. There is no muck or dirt in her. She is able to see clearly.

Just as one who walks by the fish pools in Heshbon and sees clearly the fish in the clear water, so too is her spiritual perception.

It's not that her eyes are just the "windows to her soul," but she sees clearly and discerns others.

5   Thine head upon thee is like Carmel, and the hair of thine
    head like purple; the king is held in the galleries.

One of the most magnificent things that He sees on the landscape is the majestic, strong, steadfast, enduring, and mag-

---

[65]   Robert Jamieson, A.R. Fausset & David Brown, *Jamieson, Fausset, and Brown
       Commentary* (Electronic Database by Biblesoft, Inc., 1997), Song of Solomon.

nificent Mount Carmel stretching from the Mediterranean Sea towards the southeast.

A large part of the mountain is covered with natural forest and groves that maintain their color throughout the year. It is a fruitful place.

Today, there are tourist attractions and sites in Mount Carmel. In Old Testament times, Mount Carmel is where Elijah prayed God would send fire from heaven on a wet sacrifice. Fire fell from heaven and consumed the sacrifice.

The king compares her head to Mount Carmel and her hair like purple. Purple speaks of royalty, yet one can easily determine that black hair glistening in the sun has a rich dark purple hue to it.

All the adjectives one can think of regarding Mount Carmel would be appropriate here because the writer compares her head to this mountain.

Majestic, magnificent, and pleasing to the eyes are just a few adjectives to prove that the king is captivated by His bride.

> "And now shall mine head be lifted up above mine ene-
> mies round about me: therefore, will I offer in his taber-
> nacle sacrifices of joy; I will sing, yea, I will sing praises
> unto the Lord" (Ps. 27:6).

Just as the top of Mount Carmel is facing heavenward, so too is the bride's head. Her eyes are fixed on Him. Her eyes are not on the earth and its troubles.

6 How fair and how pleasant art thou, O love, for delights!

He has made His bride beautiful. She is holy, and this is evident in her modest appearance—"fair;" "pleasant;" "O love;" and "delights!" These words are spoken from a rapturous heart. He takes great pleasure in her.

She has captivated His heart. How did she do this? Not only because of her appearance, but because she has a heart that is transformed and holy.

One might say, "She has good genes, or "good looking parents"; but true holiness has changed her completely.

When one's heart is transformed to be like Jesus, one's countenance changes.

> Lord, when you transform a Pilgrim, they become more in love with You.
> Their countenance is often altered as they serve from Your point of view.
>
> Lord, when our countenances are transformed, folk are attracted by Your Love.
> Help us to be consistently faithful while gaining Your Wisdom from above.
>
>

7 This thy stature is like to a palm tree, and thy breasts to clusters of grapes.

He looks at her from head to foot and compares her to the palm tree. And as a palm tree has fruit, so too He sees her breasts as sweet fruit.

"The righteous shall flourish like the palm tree" (Ps. 92:12).

The palm tree is a picture of a righteous person. The palm tree is straight and not twisted. It rises straight towards heaven.

> As the palm trees sway in the breezes, may my life bring refreshing from You.
> May my branches offer shelter and blessing as fruit produced offers nourishment too.
>
> The palm tree stretches towards heaven. May my life like the palm tree grow.
> So that folk around me who are observing, realize it's a privilege my Lord to know.
>
>

8 I said, I will go up to the palm tree, I will take hold of the boughs thereof: now also thy breasts shall be as clusters of the vine, and the smell of thy nose like apples;

Love satisfies the soul. It is the joy of two hearts coming together[66] and embracing. Here is a picture of the embrace.

He has likened her to a palm tree, tall, righteous, and elegant. And here, He takes a hold of her boughs, her branches. The branches of the palm tree are at the top of the tree.

He has likened her breasts to grapes of the vine that bear fruit and are pleasant to look at. He compares her to the palm, the vine, and the apple tree.

Have we lost the simple joy of viewing a tree of beauty? Have we become a high-tech person who doesn't walk outside, works from a desk, and watches television for entertainment?

Let's take some time to view the beauty of nature and reflect on these verses in the Song of Solomon.

Her mouth is sweet, and her breath is sweet like apples. Not only does she not have bad breath, but this also speaks of her purity.

To have breath like the smell of apples means that her words are also sweet. "Out of the abundance of the heart, the mouth speaks" (Matt. 12:3b).

Her heart and her belly are solely for Him, and her sweetness spoken in kind words.

---

66 Carl Friedrich Keil and Franz Delitzsch, *Commentary on the Old Testament: New Updated Edition*, Electronic Database, (Peabody, MA: Hendrickson, 1996), Song of Solomon.

9 And the roof of thy mouth like the best wine for my beloved, that goeth down sweetly, causing the lips of those that are asleep to speak.

This is such a picture of holiness, such a picture of love. Her mouth is speaking words of love. She is filled with the Spirit.

> "And be not drunk with wine, wherein is excess; but be filled with the Spirit; Speaking to yourselves in psalms and hymns and spiritual songs, singing and making melody in your heart to the Lord" (Eph. 5:18, 19).

So what rolls off your lips? How sweet is your palate to your beloved Lord? Sweet communion and sweet fellowship are like the best wine.

Lord, may the words of my mouth create blessing.
May the tone of my speech represent You.
May the wisdom found in my vocabulary
Offer encouragement in all that I do!

Words are an important part of life's fellowship.
Fellowship can nurture lost, wounded souls.
Lord, give us wisdom in our regular fellowship.
May witnessing become our true social goal!

The Shulamite Bride

10 I am my beloved's, and his desire is toward me.

There are no distractions. Sweet communion with the Lord means that we have chosen to set aside the worldly entertainment. Our delight in Him satisfies more than anything else the world has to offer.

Let us not grieve the Holy Spirit, pushing Him back, making Him wait until we have had our fill of earthly pleasures. If you are held in the clutches of too much television viewing or internet browsing and gaming, ask the Holy Spirit to help you. Come early in the morning and spend time with the Lord. His desire is towards you.

"O taste and see that the *Lord* is good: blessed is the man that trusteth in him" (Ps. 34:8).

"O fear the *Lord*, ye his saints: for there is no want to them that fear him" (Ps. 34:9).

"…but they that seek the *Lord* shall not want any good thing" (Ps. 34:10(b)).

Take delight in Him; He takes delight in you.

11 Come, my beloved, let us go forth into the field; let us lodge in the villages.

These are sweet words, "Come, my beloved." She has confidence. Not only does she belong to Him, but also He belongs to her.

The "field" is the country, and she longs to return to the country, possibly to the place of her home.

The Shulamite knows and recognizes Him as king and herself as queen, yet she longs to take Him from the hustle and bustle of the city to the quietness of the country. She wants Him to take her on a vacation or on a retreat.

She wants His full attention, His full undivided attention. She desires, if you will, that His eyes are not glazed over with work and business matters, and she knows that if she can bid Him to come to the country on a vacation, then she will have His undivided attention.

To have the undivided attention of a loved one,
Is a privilege rarely offered to but a few.
Making time to be alone with our Beloved
Is what the Lord really wants us to do.

To have your Beloved's undivided attention,
To have no distractions all around,
Offers spiritual growth and equipping
Why not try it without any other sound?

Come apart and wait in total silence.
Try worshipful adoration, God's Way.
Alone and in love with your Beloved
Is refreshingly available every day.

12 Let us get up early to the vineyards; let us see if the vine flourish, whether the tender grape appear, and the pomegranates bud forth: there will I give thee my loves.

The Shulamite earnestly seeks Him to come immediately to the country, to the villages apart from Jerusalem.

It is springtime.

Last year, I traveled to the French countryside for three weeks. The first two weeks, it was dark and rainy; but at the start of the third week, the sun broke through the clouds; and suddenly, color popped on the trees and the vines. Leaves sprung forth on every tree and vine. Places we had driven by were now lush with green buds on the vines. The vineyards came to life. Spring had sprung. It was magnificent.

The little town where we stayed, Joyeuse, is in the Ardèche department in the Auvergne-Rhône-Alpes in southern France. Joyeuse means joyfully in English. The small town is no more than a few blocks in length and somewhat dreary in appearance. But when the dark brown trees budded – suddenly the darkness was replaced with bright green.

It was life-giving to view Joyeuse and the surrounding countryside. The dark brown vineyards along the roadside flourished brilliantly with life.

The Shulamite has much love to pour out on her beloved. She desires to go to the country with Him and experience the joy of springtime.

13 The mandrakes give a smell, and at our gates are all manner of pleasant fruits, new and old, which I have laid up for thee, O my beloved.

The Shulamite has stored fruit, old and new, at the door to her family home.[67] The old fruit she had prepared in the past, the new fruit recently, but all that she has she has saved for Him.

---

[67] Carl Friedrich Keil and Franz Delitzsch, *Commentary on the Old Testament: New Updated Edition*, Electronic Database, (Peabody, MA: Hendrickson, 1996), Song of Solomon.

All that I have,

All that I am,

All I should ever be,

I cannot repay the love debt I owe,

I surrender to thee. (Author Unknown)

The fragrance of the mandrake flowers permeates the air. Two times the mandrake is mentioned in the Bible. The root of this plant has a narcotic quality, but she is not talking about the root here, but the fragrance of the flower.

Everything she possesses belongs to Him; there is nothing that she possesses that does not. She has given both her past and her future to Him—both her old fruit and her new fruit. She was prepared for His coming.

Past ministry with its joys and sorrows
Offered fruit to glean for the Lord.
Now yesterday's fruit has multiplied
Watching fresh fruit come on board.

Lord, as we prepare for Your Coming
May we keep our lamps all trimmed and bright.
Everything we possess belongs to You.
May fresh fruit now be in our sight.

Let us prepare for Your Coming.
Your arrival could happen very soon.
Keep us alert to the signs of the times.
May all our instruments also be in tune.

Notes

Chapter 8

1   O that thou wert as my brother that sucked the breasts of
my mother! when I should find thee without, I would kiss
thee; yea, I should not be despised.

The Shulamite desires intimacy with her beloved like the
closeness of family, possibly what she desired within her own
family and did not have with her own brothers and sisters.

When she would find Him outside, she would bid Him to
come in with a kiss.

He has transformed her inwardly, and now, she desires that
He transform her outwardly. She has experienced close communion with Him and sweet fellowship with Him, and she wel-
comes Him with a kiss of affection to closeness. She desires to
give her all to Him.

She bids Him come to the sweet intimate place of a close
family relationship.

2   I would lead thee, and bring thee into my mother's house,
who would instruct me: I would cause thee to drink of
spiced wine of the juice of my pomegranate.

She leads Him back to her mother's house. It is where she
grew up, and the only house she had. There, she had labored

and grown pomegranates and had prepared in advance a special wine.

She is prepared for His visit. Her pomegranate juice, properly aged with added spices, is now wine. Her labor in her earlier years has paid off; the wine is fit to drink.

She presents Him the gift of her home and her wine, representative of her heart and her labor. This is her best gift.

Is the Lord welcome in your home? Whether it be your home or the home of your parents, is He welcome? What is the atmosphere in your home? What is the spiritual climate?

When He enters your home, He brings, love, joy, peace, patience, kindness, goodness, tenderness, and self-control.

And there she will be instructed by Him. Are you open for instruction?

3   His left hand should be under my head, and his right hand should embrace me.

His protection and love embrace you. Rest in His love. Give your complete self to Him, and you will never regret it. Once you have tasted of His love, nothing else will satisfy you. Abandon yourself to Him. Give Him all. (See also Song 2:6.)

> Abandon yourself to your Beloved. Enjoy His tender Embrace.
>
> Let Him lead and protect you. His Peace you can never replace.
>
>

4   I charge you, O daughters of Jerusalem, that ye stir not up, nor awake my love, until he please.

The bride desires to hear His last words before He sleeps and His first words when He awakes. No one else should awaken Him. He is with her. While He is asleep, He is not about His kingly duties. He belongs entirely to her, His bride, and she will safeguard His rest.

There is nothing that draws her away; there are no other attractions. She guards her communion with Him, and even while He sleeps, she desires to be the first eye-to-eye contact when He awakens. She wants to hear His first words. She guards Him from all others that may seek to call Him away from her.

> At night when you are sleeping. What does your Beloved say to you?
>
> Cherish all the words that are spoken. Write down His words to review.
>
> Perhaps He offers words of wisdom. Perhaps He offers approval to you.
>
> Maybe He encourages and blesses? Remember His Words are unique for you.
>
>

The Bridegroom King

5 Who is this that cometh up from the wilderness, leaning upon her beloved? I raised thee up under the apple tree: there thy mother brought thee forth: there she brought thee forth that bare thee.

The wilderness is a picture of your old nature where you have learned who you are and who you are not without your beloved by your side. You have come to know yourself, and you have learned that your greatest delight is to lean on your beloved. You walk in His strength. You have given up your other "supports" to fully trust in Him.

The tender time of being "raised up under the apple tree" pertains to us all, yet not all of us have had a tender upbringing. Some of my friends have had a tumultuous upbringing.

Yet, there is an absolutely most tender time in everyone's past and that is the day of salvation and the infilling of the Holy Spirit. There, we are "marked" as His and experience the joy of new life in Christ Jesus. That is the day we are "raised up." Through the seasons and the years, the bride has learned to lean on her beloved, and He supplies her every need.

Raised up, with His life, His blood flowing through our veins, new life—And this is our hope, the hope of glory. We not only are saved from our sins but also experience new life in Christ Jesus. What Adam and Eve lost in the Garden of Eden is restored to us through Jesus Christ's death and resurrection.

The Shulamite Bride

6 Set me as a seal upon thine heart, as a seal upon thine arm: for love is strong as death; jealousy is cruel as the grave: the coals thereof are coals of fire, which hath a most vehement flame.

A seal today is made with melted wax, which is sometimes placed on the back of an envelope, with the stamp (possibly an emblem or initial) used to seal the envelope.

In the time of Solomon, a seal was made with clay and had the emblem or mark of the king in it. It is similar to a signature, giving one full authority from the king. Also, in the past, a signet ring made a seal. Whoever had the ring had the authority of the king. When the king died, He would pass His signet ring to the next heir to the throne, signifying that this heir was to become the new king.

The Shulamite asks, "Set me as a seal on thine heart… upon thine arm." A seal on His heart means that His desires and affections are for her alone. The Shulamite desires that she is sealed in His heart. She desires His undivided love.

"…love is as strong as death;" (Song 8:6b). In her passionate love for Him, she testifies how love is stronger than death, and jealousy (a powerful component of love) is as cruel as the grave.

The love that will not let her go, the love that *holds the reigns* within her, the love whose passion has an unquenchable flame—this is the love she has abandoned herself to; and nothing, not even the hottest flame, will cause her love to weaken or come to an end.

Below is a gospel song entitled *Something Within*, written by Lucie Eddie Campbell, an African American woman, and first sung in 1919. It is no doubt that Campbell knew she was sealed in her King Jesus's heart, as He was sealed in her heart.

> Something within me that holdeth the reins.
> Something within me that vanishes pain,
> Something within me I cannot explain,
> All I know there is something within. (Lucie Eddie Campbell)

And updated version of the same song is also provided below.

It's Jesus within me, He's holding the reins,

It's Jesus within me, He vanishes pain,

It's Jesus within me, O praise His Name,

All I know, praise the Lord, it is Jesus within. (Unknown Author)

7   Many waters cannot quench love, neither can the floods drown it: if a man would give all the substance of his house for love, it would utterly be contemned.

Nothing can destroy pure love. "When the enemy shall come in like a flood, the Spirit of the Lord shall lift up a standard against him" (Isa. 59:19b). The love of God is so rich and pure. Whether it be coals of fire or a flood of water, nothing can quench His love. All the comforts of your life and all the "substance of" your house cannot hold a candle to this love.

He doesn't seek our things, our possessions, but our heart. You cannot substitute, trade, or pay for this love with everything you own as these things would be treated with scorn, disdain, or contempt. These things are unworthy of consideration.

Let us "love God with all [our] heart, soul, mind and strength" (Mark 12:30). Let us give ourselves completely to Him.

8   We have a little sister, and she hath no breasts: what shall we do for our sister in the day when she shall be spoken for?

The Shulamite speaks what her brothers may have asked her while in her parent's home.[68] She loves her sister and desires that she is protected for marriage and that her innocence is guarded.

Is it possible that her little sister represents those who are not yet ready for marriage and unable to give life because she "hath no breasts"? The elder sister, Shulamite is the one who is concerned for her little sister and prays that she will be protected for marriage. Is little sister representative of those who have not yet found Jesus Christ as Lord and Savior?

If we are truly the bride, do we have a love and concern for little sister who is not yet prepared?

> Lord, You know all about little sisters.
> You know those who are not ready to go.
> You know how we want them to find You.
> But nothing we've done seems to flow.
>
> As an elder brother or sister
> Prepare us to speak out for You.
> No matter the day or the hour
> May we show them the way to You.

---

[68]   *Barnes' Notes*, Electronic Database, Biblesoft Electronic Database, 1997.

9   If she be a wall, we will build upon her a palace of silver: and
if she be a door, we will enclose her with boards of cedar.

Little sister's sacred honor is to be protected with silver or
cedar. If she were strong like a wall, her brothers would build a
palace of silver to keep her until she is married. If she is acces-
sible like a door, her brothers would protect her with strong
fragrant cedar. Her beauty and immaturity would be protected.

Silver represents the redemption of Jesus Christ. To be built
with silver is her defense against those who would try to take
her off course. Hence, her brothers would build a palace of silver to keep her until she is married. Barnes relates that she is
"stedfast in chastity and virtue, one on whom no light advances
can be made, then let us honor and reward her."[69]

If she is still moveable, like a door, she needs to learn of Jesus
and His love for her; His grace, and His characteristics. A wall
is firm, whereas a door is moveable. Either way, plans are made
for her protection.

---

[69]   Albert Barnes, *Barnes' Notes*, (Electronic Database by Biblesoft, Inc., 1997),
Song of Solomon.

A loved one still needs Jesus.
A friend is lost in their sin.
Whenever we are led by the Spirit
May a decision by them come in.

Keep us vigilant and faithful to win them.
Keep us alert to speak God's true Word.
May they come to accept the Master
Eternal life is the best news ever heard.

10 I am a wall, and my breasts like towers: then was I in his eyes as one that found favour.

The bride explains that she is a wall (not a door), and as a result of her innocence and purity, she has been crowned as queen. The king found favor in her. She has lived her life as an example.

Her breasts as towers represent her defense. She is a wall, and her breasts are like towers.[70] The Shulamite has grown and has given her all to her bridegroom. She encourages her sister to also grow to maturity like she has and to trust her beloved.

---

[70]   Matthew Henry, *Matthew Henry's Commentary on the Whole Bible: New Modern Edition*, (Electronic Database by Biblesoft, Inc.: Hendrickson Publishers, Inc., 1991), Song of Solomon.

Little sister represents those who have not yet found the bridegroom.

She encourages her little sister to find favor, like she did, in His eyes.

Her beloved is her Lord. Protect your sacred honor and give yourself to Him entirely. Give everything you have to Him. You will never regret it. Totally abandon yourself to Him and His ways. You will never leave Him once you have truly experienced your Lord.

11 Solomon had a vineyard at Baal-hamon; he let out the vineyard unto keepers; every one for the fruit thereof was to bring a thousand pieces of silver.

Solomon (*peaceful*) is a type of Christ. His vineyard that He had at Baal-hamon is a representative of the vineyard He has entrusted to us. His vineyard is a type of the church. He has entrusted us as keepers of His vineyard, and He keeps a watchful eye over His vineyard.

Although the Shulamite does not keep her own vineyard (Song 1:6), she will, with all diligence, pay the workers in this vineyard. The profit of the vineyard belongs to Solomon or, as better understood, Christ. He is to receive the first fruits of our labor. His workers will receive a just sum.

12 My vineyard, which is mine, is before me: thou, O Solomon, must have a thousand, and those that keep the fruit thereof two hundred.

Granted by Solomon, the vineyard is "mine" (the bride's vineyard), and she is given the power over it. She is not focused on making a profit for herself, but the proceeds are for His glory.

The keepers of the vineyard are rewarded with pay for their service.

The bride of Christ is His church. The vineyard is the world. Let us not be slack in the care of His vineyard. All is done for the bridegroom, and your love for Him allows you to work and give of yourself freely.

Surrender all you have to the lover of your soul.

The Bridegroom King

13 Thou that dwellest in the gardens, the companions hearken to thy voice: cause me to hear it.

The bridegroom wants to hear from the bride's voice—her words and her praise from her lips that originates in her heart. "A good man out of the good treasure of his heart bringeth forth that which is good; and an evil man out of the evil treasure of his heart bringeth forth that which is evil: for of the abundance of the heart his mouth speaketh" (Luke 6:45).

There is a "longing" and a "desire" written of here—a longing to be with one another. Yet the bridegroom is leaving her for a while.

Her companions will hear her voice. She will instruct them to follow after the King. She will remain to tend His garden with a cheerful heart until He returns.

He desires to hear our wants, our prayers. We should just as easily pray to Him as we talk to our friends.

The Shulamite Bride

14 Make haste, my beloved, and be thou like to a roe or to a young hart upon the mountains of spices.

He has already told her to speak regularly to Him, and this is her reply: "Return quickly!"

You labor for your Lord. You speak kind words about Him and to Him. Your desire is for Him to return.

She is happy. He has left before and returned suddenly, and so this time, she knows He will return speedily.

Is your heart desirous of His return? Or are you tied to the things of the earth so much that you fear His return? If you truly long for His return and have made Him Lord of your life, you are ready and waiting expectantly.

Speak of His return. Look for His return. Let your affections truly be towards Him.

(See also Songs 4:6 and 2:17.)

And now we have read the Song of Solomon.
We have waited and watched as the Lord led.
Lord keep us aware of Your Fresh Anointing
Because of what the Beloved Lover has said.

You loved us enough to become our substitute.
You loved us enough to provide.
Thank You for the future we have with the Bridegroom.
It will be our privilege to constantly abide.

Notes

Bibliography

Adam Clarke's Commentary, Electronic Database. Copyright 1996 by Biblesoft, Inc.

Barnes' Notes, Electronic Database. Copyright 1997 by Biblesoft, Inc.

Bernard of Clairvaux, *Life and Works of Saint Bernard: Eighty Six Sermons on The Song of Solomon,* Ed. John Mabillon, London: John Hodges, 1896.

Bernard of Clairvaux. *Song of Solomon.* Minneapolis, Minnesota: Klock & Klock Christian Publishers, Inc., 1984.

Bickle, Mike. Loving Jesus: The First Commandment Established in First Place. Sermon presented at New Life Church, Virginia Beach, VA. 31 July 2016.

Bloch, Ariel, and Chana Bloch. *The Song of Songs.* Los Angeles: University of California Press, 1995.

Burrowes, George. *A Commentary on the Song of Solomon.* Carlisle, Pennsylvania: The Banner of Truth Trust, 1853.

Cahn, Jonathan. *The Book of Mysteries.* Lake Mary, Florida: Frontline, 2016.

Calvin, John. *The Institutes of the Christian Religion.* Edited by Henry Beveridge. Seattle, WA: Pacific Publishing Studio, 2011.

Fausset, Andrew Robert. *Fausset's Bible Dictionary, Electronic Database.* Copyright 1996 by Biblesoft, Inc.

Gill, John. *An Exposition of the Song of Solomon.* Grand Rapids, Michigan: Sovereign Grace Publishers, 1971.

Guyon, Jeanne. *Song of Songs: Explanations and Reflections Regarding the Deeper Christian Life.* Jacksonville, FL: The Seed Sowers, 1990.

John of Ford. *Sermons of the Final Verses of the Song of Songs.* Kalamazoo, Michigan: Cistercian Publications, 1977.

Hadley, E. C. *The Song of Solomon.* Danville, Illinois: Grace & Truth, 1975.

Jamieson, Fausset, and Brown Commentary. Electronic Database. Copyright 1996 by Biblesoft, Inc.

Jastrow, Morris, Jr. *The Song of Songs: Being A Collection of Love Lyrics of Ancient Palestine.* Philadelphia: J. B. Lippincott Company, 1921.

Keil, Carl Friedrich, and Franz Delitzsch. *Commentary on The Song of Songs and Ecclesiastes.* Grand Rapids, Michigan: Wm. B. Eerdmans Publishing Company, 1950.

Keil, Carl Friedrich, and Franz Delitzsch. *Commentary on the Old Testament: New Updated Edition.* Electronic Database. Peabody, MA: Hendrickson, 1996.

Leiman, Sid Z. *The Canonization of Hebrew Scripture: The Talmudic and Midrashic Evidence, 2ⁿᵈ Ed.* New Haven:

Transactions of the Connecticut Academy of Arts and Sciences, 1991.

Lewis, C. S. *Surprised by Joy*. New York, NY: Harper Collins Publishers, 1955.

Lewis, C. S., *Letters to Malcolm: Chiefly on Prayer*, San Diego, CA: Harvest House Publishing, 1964.

Luther, Martin. *History of the Great Reformation of the Sixteenth Century in Germany, Switzerland & C*. Translated by J. H. Merle D'Aubigne. NY: Robert Carter, 1843.

Matthew Henry's Commentary on the Whole Bible: New Modern Edition. Electronic Database. Copyright 1991 by Biblesoft, Inc.

McGee, J. Vernon. *Guidelines for the Understanding of Scripture: Song of Solomon*. Through the Bible Radio Network. TN: Thomas Nelson, 1988.

Penn-Lewis, Jessie. *The Hidden Ones: Union with Christ Traced in the Song of Songs*. Fort Washington, PA: Christian Literature Crusade, 1951.

Renan, Ernest. *The Song of Songs*. Paternoster Square, E. C., London: Mathieson & Co., 1860.

Saint Ambrose of Milan. *De Fide and De Spiritu Sancto*. Morrisville, NC: Pilgrimage House Press, 2010.

Schmidt, Gwen R. *The Marriage Song*. Singapore: Creative Service, 1962.

Taylor, James Hudson. *Union and Communion: Or Thoughts on the Song of Solomon.* Philadelphia: The China Inland Mission, 1914.

Thompson Chain-Reference Bible. Indianapolis, IN: Kirkbride Bible Co., 1998.

The NET Bible First Edition Notes, copyright 1997-2016 by Biblical Studies Press, L.L.C., 2006.

The Strongest Strong's Exhaustive Concordance of the Bible. Grand Rapids: Zondervan Publishing Company, 2001.

The Wycliffe Bible Commentary, Electronic Database, Copyright 1962 by Moody Press.

Wiseman, D. J. *The Song of Solomon: An Introduction and Commentary.* Edited by G. Lloyd Carr. Downers Grove, Illinois: Intervarsity Press, 1930.

W. E. Vine, Merrill F. Unger, and William White, Jr. *Vine's Complete Expository Dictionary of Old and New Testament Words.* Nashville, TN: Thomas Nelson, 1996.

Reference Works

Adam Clarke's Commentary, Electronic Database. Copyright 1996 by Biblesoft, Inc.

Barnes' Notes, Electronic Database. Copyright 1997 by Biblesoft, Inc.

Jamieson, Fausset, and Brown Commentary. Electronic Database. Copyright 1996 by Biblesoft, Inc.

Keil, Carl Friedrich, and Franz Delitzsch. *Commentary on the Old Testament: New Updated Edition*. Electronic Database. Peabody, MA: Hendrickson, 1996.

Matthew Henry's Commentary on the Whole Bible: New Modern Edition. Electronic Database. Copyright 1991 by Biblesoft, Inc.

The Wycliffe Bible Commentary, Electronic Database, Copyright 1962 by Moody Press.

About the Author

Lorrie Bergman Belke, born and raised in Ontario, Canada, is the daughter of Rev. Earl and Doreen Bergman. Following graduation from Regent University she was blessed with the opportunity to be able to stay home and home school during the day and teach college classes in the evenings. Presently she is pursuing a doctorate in biblical studies.

Lorrie and her husband, Tom, and son, Benjamin, reside in Chesapeake, Virginia.

Marlene D. Bergman is a former teacher, seminar speaker, and businesswoman. A few years ago, Marnie (as she prefers to be called) experienced a personal and emotional healing. During that time, the Lord suddenly gifted her with the "sacred surprise" of a poetic pen! Marnie lives in Ontario, Canada, with her husband Jerry. They have a son, daughter, and three grandchildren.

CPSIA information can be obtained
at www.ICGtesting.com
Printed in the USA
BVHW03s2154210818
525269BV00001B/26/P